TECHNOLOGY, THEOLOGY, and the IDEA OF PROGRESS

DAVID H. HOPPER

WESTMINSTER/JOHN KNOX PRESS
LOUISVILLE, KENTUCKY

Scripture quotations from the Revised Standard Version of the Bible are copyrighted 1946, 1952, © 1971, 1973 by the Division of Christian Education of the National Council of the Churches of Christ in the U.S.A. and are used by permission.

Excerpts from *The Heavenly City of the Eighteenth-Century Philosophers*, by Carl Becker, are copyright © 1932 Yale University Press, renewed 1960 by Carl L. Becker, and are used by permission of the publisher.

Excerpts from *Progress and Power*, by Carl Becker, are copyright © 1936, 1949, by Alfred A. Knopf, Inc., and renewed 1964 by Frederick D. Becker. Reprinted by permission of Alfred A. Knopf, Inc.

Excerpts from *The Idea of Progress*, by J. B. Bury, are copyright © 1932 by The Macmillan Co. and copyright © 1960 by William Beard and Mrs. Miriam B. Vagts. Used by permission of Dover Publications, Inc.

Lines from the poem "To the Memory of Sir Isaac Newton," by James Thomson, are from J. Logie Robertson, ed., *The Complete Poetical Works of James Thomson* (Oxford: Oxford University Press, 1908), and are used by permission of Oxford University Press.

Excerpts from articles printed in *The New York Times* are copyright © 1983, 1984, 1986, 1988 by The New York Times Company. Reprinted by permission.

Book design by Publishers' WorkGroup

First edition

Published by Westminster/John Knox Press
Louisville, Kentucky

PRINTED IN THE UNITED STATES OF AMERICA
9 8 7 6 5 4 3 2 1

Library of Congress Cataloging-in-Publication Data

Hopper, David H. (David Henry), 1927–
    Technology, theology, and the idea of progress / David H. Hopper.
— 1st ed.
        p.   cm.
    Includes bibliographical references.
    ISBN 0-664-25203-6

    1. Technology—Religious aspects—Christianity.   2. Progress—Religious aspects—Christianity.   I. Title.
BR115.T42H66 1991
261.5′6—dc20   90-24106

TECHNOLOGY, THEOLOGY, and the IDEA OF PROGRESS

Consider the subtleness of the sea; how its
most dreaded creatures glide under water,
unapparent for the most part, and
treacherously hidden beneath
the loveliest tints of azure.

Herman Melville
Moby-Dick

CONTENTS

PREFACE

On a visit to Macalester College in the spring of 1981, Stephen Toulmin, the historian and philosopher of science, offered this comment at one point, "Some questions are too important to be left to the experts." I forget the precise context of his remark, but I had become increasingly involved with the question of technology at the time and it is with this question that I have associated the comment ever since. Toulmin's remark has served as one of the goads for this book. I believe that technology and its increasing impact upon all of our lives is too important a question to be left to the experts.

One of the problems in trying to deal with this subject, however, is its vastness and also its subtlety, a subtlety that has allowed technology to pervade all corners of our lives without a struggle, on our part, to understand how this has happened. We often are not aware of the dominating role it has come to play, though this seems somewhat inconceivable! Awareness of this aspect of technology is occurring now, however, for growing numbers of people who are confronted with decisions neither they nor their parents were ever before called upon to make. I believe it came most sharply into focus for me when I began teaching a course, some ten years ago, entitled "Technology and Ethics." In this course, I came to realize that ethically speaking we scurry here and there picking up the pieces of what technology has left behind. We have been left to face ethical problems which we never would have chosen for ourselves "if we had known." My conclusion was that we have not sufficiently understood, we have not properly "pictured," the phenomenon that technology has become for all of us in this last decade of the twentieth century.

Of course numbers of important and helpful volumes have been written on the history of technology, on the phenomenon of technology as "system," on its nature as a social and political phenomenon. By "picturing" I mean an imaging of the phenomenon that allows us to move about with an understanding in our heads, and allows us to think about it in our workplaces and in front of our television sets, not just in our classrooms or before a printed page.

I am reminded at this point of an aspect of Western religious history during the Reformation period. Martin Luther, of course, had the great advantage over earlier religious reformers of having access to the printing press, which enabled him to reach more readers more rapidly than any of his predecessors had been able to do. Literacy itself, however, was limited and thus most of Luther's early pamphlets and sermons were accompanied by woodcuts: his message was quite literally pictured.

There are no pictures in this book. Literacy, of course, is much more widespread than ever before: everyone knows that. But I do not think the need of picturing has diminished. Ideas, accurate and truthful, must be framed to take root in people's lives if ideas and people are to have an impact, if history itself is to have meaning. I believe that the effort to picture the role and function of technology is the crying need of our time, and it is this need which I have tried to address. This book actually offers an argument, a way of understanding technology, which, if successful, can instill a critical distance to our viewing. In the end I do not think any of us can be satisfied with just another learned, or not so learned, discussion of technology—or with what one historian has described as "a Renaissance attitude" which "creates sociologically the aristocracy of culture and the salon and for the rest pays homage to might and power."[1] I believe that we must move in the direction of a critical, informed knowledge of technology and the role it now plays in our lives. I express my bias when I say that I do not think that technology should be allowed simply to run its course. I argue in what follows that we need to sharpen our sense for the issues, reexamine our commitments, and ask ourselves again, What counts?

Let me spell out the "imaging," the argument, that lies ahead. I begin, in chapter 1, by stating the problem. I draw here upon two pictures that are already etched in our memories and are likely to remain there in the years to come: the recent events of Chernobyl and Challenger.[2] I point up the peculiar demand that these two events represent for the educational enterprise: the simultaneous distancing and cultivation of familiarity. In chapter 2 I present what I propose as the most helpful historical perspective on the course of technology, the development of the idea of Progress. Here the argument rehearses the emergence of the idea of Progress along the lines pursued by the historian J. B. Bury—a picturing necessary to avoid the assumption that Progress and technology are essentially a tandem, ages-old phenomenon. A recent major study by Robert Nisbet has drawn this latter, false image and it demands correction. In citing a 1920 against a 1980 study, I suggest in passing that with the liberal arts it is *not* the case that the more recent is necessarily the better.

Chapter 3 projects the image of the decline of the political idea of Progress and the technological usurpation of the idea. Here an explanation is offered for how this has come about. I propose that disillusion with political progress, along with the lust for power, has been chiefly responsible for the peculiar dominance of technology in our late-twentieth-century world. Chapter 4 describes the dubious effort to claim political values (democracy, freedom) for the technological enterprise. Chapter 5 rejects the simplistic charge of religious culpability for the technologically induced environmental crisis. This chapter also asserts, however, that the theological response to the "technological crisis" has been woefully inadequate. Chapter 6, "Summation and Theological Postscript," suggests that the argument offered in these chapters makes clearer the "meaning" of present-day events and calls for the *critical*, responsible involvement of the reader in the events of our time.

In presenting the discussion outlined here I have seen fit to quote human voices somewhat more than customary. Not only the thought but also the human voices that express the thoughts are basic to the argument that follows.

A brief word should be said at the start about the term "technology." By technology I mean what most others have meant by the term: the invention and development of tools and machines, all the great variety of mechanical devices which the human community has developed in its struggle to control and exploit the forces of nature. But human manipulation and control have been extended beyond nature to encompass the human community as well. Here others, especially Jacques Ellul, have utilized the term "technique" to refer to the varied phenomena of advertising, propaganda, psychological coercion, and the design of organizational structures which intend "efficiency," economic and social control. If there is anything innovative in the present discussion's use of the term "technology," it lies in an exploration of the "addictive" character of technology: its capacity to afford immense satisfaction and stimulation; its capacity to command human acquiescence and commitment; its ability to provide an ongoing but limited sense of purpose and meaning for human life.

In closing I want to express gratitude for my long-term liberal arts education, which began years ago at Yale College and has continued over the years of my teaching at Macalester College. What I have valued in my teaching-learning experience at Macalester has been the tolerance of exploratory discussions with students and faculty colleagues—at times in "improbable" interdisciplinary courses which challenge the adequacy of our "safe" academic expertise. In courses that skirted the boundaries of a discipline, conversations were initiated, students engaged, instructors instructed. Along with the many students to whom I owe much, I want to thank two faculty friends who have taught with me and who have shared their stimulating, contrary views on "the things that count": Jeremiah Reedy in Classics and Vassant Sukhatme in Economics.

I owe a debt to the National Endowment of the Humanities for the opportunity to participate in two of its Summer Seminars for College Teachers, one at Yale in 1976 with Hans Frei and one at the University of Maryland in 1983 with Steven Brush. A 1977 seminar sponsored by the University of Chicago on the theme "Technology and Values" also proved to be a rich learning experience.

Special thanks are due to Mrs. Peggy B. Stivers for major help in the typing of this manuscript. My three daughters, Sara, Katy, and Rachel, have served as a special inspiration for me.

St. Paul, Minnesota   D. H. H.

1

HAS TECHNOLOGY BECOME
OUR HISTORY?

During the summer of 1986 I was part of a study group devoted to the theme "Technology in Tension with Human Values." In the course of a discussion I asked the group members, "What major events in the past year have most gripped you as a person?" I should note that the members of the study group were generally well informed on social and political issues, so I was somewhat surprised at the answers they gave. Three events were cited: the Challenger disaster, the bombing of Libya, and the Chernobyl disaster. I then made the observation that two of the three events were essentially technological events in contrast to political events. The discussion that followed underlined the point which has now become obvious to more and more people everywhere: that while technology has provided us with many material benefits, it is also commanding more and more of our lives. I came away from the discussion with another question fixed in my mind: the question that serves as the title of this chapter, Has technology become our history?

The question asks simply this: Has technology come to embody our chief values—the things we most want out of life? Does it not, in fact, represent our basic commitment? This is a large question, a cultural question, a question about America as a nation and people, but also about the nations of Europe and Asia as well—the world.[1]

Technological innovation proceeds at an ever more rapid pace with little regard for the long-term social impact of any given innovation or the political purposes and values a particular nation or people may embrace. To be sure, there are growing efforts at resistance from environmentalists concerned about the degradation of the natural environment and also from some religious traditions that seek to preserve the social structure and religious meanings of an earlier time, but by and large the pace of technological innovation and its spread are little altered by these efforts. Some natural and perhaps cultural preserves may be carved out for alternative patterns of life, but the expansion of technology into most corners of public and private life continues apace, seemingly inevitably.[2] Thus, as a people, we find that we are increasingly confronted with questions that, deep down, we do not want to ask: When do I decide to let a loved one die? What about my own death, the quality of life at the end and its cost? What of the possibility of global destruction, nuclear war? As a result of technology how vulnerable have we become to our own mistakes and weaknesses? Where are the guidelines, the markers, by which we can chart our way in a world dominated by technological change and the ongoing quest for power which technology generates?

Trained in theology, Christian thought, I remain committed to the belief that the focus of meaning is the question of God and the cross, the figure of Jesus preserved in the biblical narratives, but I don't think I am naive about how these affirmations of meaning fit into the affairs of our world. We in the West measure our years by the Christ event; we date the flow of history by that event. Is this the real focus of meaning in our time? It may have been at an earlier period in history, but is it now?

From where I live and work, I can look out over the skyline of the city of Minneapolis and mark the monuments of meaning which dominate that skyline. These monuments are essentially financial and technological. The sister city of St. Paul differs a little on this point. Years ago the Catholic community chose the high bluff overlooking the city as the site for its cathedral—a building visible in all directions. Downtown St. Paul is building still—and its new "cathedrals" of glass and steel rise in impressive grandeur. The eye moves, drifts, from the cathedral to the state capitol building, to the commercial and business center, the technological center, of the city. And the action is there.

The picture of technology's rise can be sketched in still another way. At one time in Western history the best minds of the day were attracted to my own discipline, theology. Theology, the most compelling of intellectual inquiries, was described as the "queen of the sciences." As a result of this earlier history one can trace in subsequent Christian thought a great deal of nostalgia. The haunting memory of the Middle Ages and theology's preeminence has led to frequent efforts to reclaim the world for the religious point of view. In our own time one notes a theological-philosophical effort to resuscitate metaphysics and to reconceptualize the world in such a way that everything becomes once more "religious." Paul Tillich performed such a "good work" of the mind, as has also Alfred North Whitehead and the process theologians who follow in his train. Technology, however, proceeds without pause, unaware that in theological studies and libraries it has been somehow "baptized" and "accepted" within systems of "religious meaning."[3]

Some time ago I taped to the wall over my desk a sentence—two sentences—from a 1932 work of Carl Becker, *The Heavenly City of the Eighteenth-Century Philosophers*. The statement serves as a cautionary word against theological romanticism, a warning against religious-aesthetic inclinations to establish a world apart from the actualities of history and power. Becker writes:

> In the course of eight centuries . . . (theology, philosophy and deductive logic) have fallen from their high estate. Theology, or something that goes under that name, is still kept alive by the faithful, but only by artificial respiration.[4]

It is sobering to be reminded how others look upon one's own world of meaning, how they often lack a sense for its "proper" scope and conceptualization.

Rather than a theological restoration, which aims to reclaim culture for a religious point of view, it may be better for theologians simply to exorcize this particular ghost and live with theology's diminished stature and role. Instead of doing battle for God, even a God refashioned and fitted for modern sensitivities, it may be our better role to bring the experience of religion's decline to bear upon an understanding of our times. If Carl Becker's reading of the pulse of theology can be regarded as at least somewhat exaggerated, at another place he makes a point I find to be personally compelling. He argues that

> to regard all things in their historical setting appears, indeed, to be an instructive procedure of the modern mind. We do it without thinking, because we can scarcely think at all without doing it. Historical-mindedness is so much a preconception of modern thought that we can identify a particular thing only by pointing to the various things it successively was before it became that particular thing which it will presently cease to be.[5]

Seeing things in sequence, the development and decline of ideas and institutions: this, Becker argues, is the way we moderns understand. Not logic, clothed with some sort of ultimate status, bearing a quasi-divine character, but the description and understanding of things in sequence affords us our chief claim to knowing.

If this is a fair statement of what we in the twentieth century most widely define as understanding, let me suggest that a discipline such as theology which has known its own rise and decline can serve to illumine other developments in the flow of history, the rise to prominence of other ideas and hopes—and similarly their decline. Let me propose here that what replaced religion as the focus of hope and meaning in Western culture from the seventeenth century to our own times was science, to be sure, but in a special way also politics. Science helped to enliven the political possibility in the seventeenth and eighteenth centuries but now it serves primarily the technological hope.[6]

To return to the question Has technology become our history? we are asking whether politics, like religion, is now well into its decline, serving no longer its own vision and possibilities but rather now those chiefly of technology. If one goes back to that incident described at the beginning of this chapter, the incident that called forth the question What major events in the past year have most gripped you as a person? one could argue that the answers given to that question were simply the result of happenstance, that the citing of the Challenger (January 18, 1986) and the Chernobyl (April 26, 1986) disasters was not so much a sign of the increasing dominance of technology over politics but only a matter of timing, nothing more. There is certainly some point to this contention, but a review of both events and the political, social, and "technical" responses to these events suggests that each one, in its own way, says a great deal about the role of technology in our growing global culture.

It should be clear here that by citing this instance of two technological disasters I do not mean to make an argument at the start against technology. These two events have simply had a special historical impact— at least in the year 1986—even as the landing on the moon had a special impact in the year 1969 and after, and the launching of Sputnik in 1957. Important events stir emotions, sometimes admiration and wonder, sometimes shock and anxiety. Sometimes hopes are bolstered; sometimes they are shaken and dashed. This is what we mean by history.

Of course, in the case of Challenger and Chernobyl the impact was one of shock and sorrow, fear and concern. The tragic and frightening nature of these events was felt worldwide. But, let me suggest that the two events remain paradigmatically important for what they say about the role technology has come to play in our lives. These two events deserve remembrance, scrutiny, and analysis on this account, even though their memory has already begun to fade. Let us consider the Chernobyl event first, and Challenger second.

Standing as the worst accident in the troubled history of nuclear power technology, the Chernobyl disaster was preceded by a whole series of lesser incidents around the world. This history suggested the probability that something like Chernobyl would eventually come to pass, as a result of either major technical failure, or some error in human judgment, or a combination of both. In 1980 Ronald W. Clark published a balanced discussion of the history and problems of nuclear energy, from the building and use of the bomb in World War II to the nuclear power plant accident at Three Mile Island, Pennsylvania, in

March 1979. Clark discussed the chances of a serious nuclear power accident occurring in the future.

> Release of radioactivity, the main danger in a reactor accident, is most likely to be brought about by a failure to take heat away from the reactor core, a melt-down of the core, a breaching of the protective shield, and a release into the atmosphere of lethal radioactivity. This, like any comparable nuclear disaster, would come about only after an unexpected failure of equipment, and, following that, the failure of fail-safe precautionary devices.[7]

Then Clark continued—again, one notes that these words come from the year 1980:

> When the chances of such an accident taking place are estimated the figures vary so considerably that faith in them rapidly disappears. According to the Rasmussen Report (of 1974, produced by Professor Rasmussen of the Massachusetts Institute of Technology), the chances are of one [major] accident . . . in about 200 million years of reactor operation. Even when operating reactors have risen in numbers to 1000 this would still suggest only a single accident in some 200,000 years. However, the figures give no direct information on when the one accident would take place. And an equally well-informed research report, the Ford Foundation's *Nuclear Power: Issues and Choices*, reduces the time scale by a factor of 10,000— thus bringing the latest date for a serious accident no later than the turn of the present century.[8]

What was determined statistically in the Rasmussen Report to be one accident in 200,000 years and by the Ford Foundation's study as one in twenty years, has of course, already occurred. Perhaps something worse than Chernobyl was envisioned, but the Chernobyl accident was, by all considerations, bad enough.

The *New York Times* reported on September 23, 1986, that

> the nuclear disaster at Chernobyl emitted as much long-term radiation into the world's air, topsoil and water as all the nuclear tests and bombs ever exploded, according to a new study of the April 26 Soviet accident. The study, by the Lawrence Livermore National Laboratory in California, says the Soviet reactor might even have emitted 50 percent more radioactive cesium, the primary long-term component in fallout, than have all atmospheric tests and bombs combined. Cesium does not decay into harmless substances for more than 100 years and has been associated with health effects such as cancer and genetic disease.[9]

Unlike nuclear bomb explosions which produce higher short-term radiation and damage, nuclear reactor accidents, like the one at Chernobyl, give off more long-term radioactive contaminants.

The Livermore study estimated that "more than eight tons of highly radioactive material was emitted from the accident, and some of it was deposited hundreds of miles away." "The report said that the initial steam explosion from the plant blew off its 1000 ton steel cover plate and ripped off the tops of all 1661 channels attached to the cover plate and containing nuclear fuel: Those channels became like '1600 howitzers pointed at the sky,' (said) Dr. Herbert J. C. Kouts, head of the Department of Nuclear Energy at Brookhaven National Laboratory. . . . Kouts said people miles away saw 'a fireworks display of hot radioactive material being thrown into the night sky.' "[10]

Though the Soviet Union seems to have tried at first to conceal the extent and details of the accident, it eventually turned to full disclosure. At an international conference in August 1986, almost four months after the disaster, an account of what caused the accident was finally provided.

A series of experiments were being carried out at the Chernobyl power plant to test the residual energy-producing potential of the steam turbines after a reactor was shut down. The experiment was placed under the direction of electrical engineers, not nuclear power experts. The *New York Times* account read as follows:

> The test was to be conducted at just over 20 percent power. But when the operators reduced the power to that level, they did not push a switch that would have held power there. As a result, the power dropped to 1 percent, far lower than that needed to do the test. . . . The reactor became very unstable and difficult to control partly because of certain gases such as xenon building up inside, and because of elevated temperatures of the cooling water. . . . Instead of shutting the reactor down operators raised its power to about 6 percent and held it there, although their rules called for no operation below 20 percent power because of instability. The experiment should have been terminated [at this point].
>
> In raising the power level [to 6 percent] operators kept withdrawing control rods from the core until at one point only 6 of 211 remained. At least 30 are required by the unit's operating manual. Automatic equipment to shut down and cool the reactor in an emergency was turned off, in violation of regulations, over a 24-hour period. . . . Even so, [the report] said, the reactor could have been saved up until the last 40 seconds. But at that time, four seconds after 1:23 A.M. on April 26, the operators blocked the reactor's ability to automatically shut down during the test they were about to do. They wanted to be able to repeat the test, and needed a running reactor. . . .
>
> When operators finally realized the danger 36 seconds later and tried to shut down the reactor by dropping the control rods into the core, it was too late. The unit blew apart about five seconds later. The fuel atomized. The graphite, which operates at a very high 1400 degrees Fahrenheit normally, caught fire. There were at least two explosions; the second could also have been a steam explosion, not hydrogen, as had been thought.[11]

An estimated 25 percent of the total radiation released at Chernobyl was released on the first day; the other 75 percent, over the ensuing eight days.

The assessments that took place in the aftermath of the accident laid major responsibility for the disaster on human error. Dr. Kouts, the American nuclear expert who helped summarize the Soviet report, offered the comment: "The operators got swelled heads. . . . They thought they could do anything to this reactor. That should be a lesson for everyone."[12] Analyses of this aspect of the accident identified a sequence of six errors in human judgment.[13] All the errors in judgment were quite rational within the framework of the turbine experiment but they violated the safety rules for the operation of the reactor itself. The 382-page Soviet report, released August 22, declared: "The reactor builders had not foreseen a situation of 'premeditated diversions of technical protection facilities' by operators, coupled with violations of rules. Such a set of circumstances was thought to be 'impossible.' " "The report called for improvements in training and for international cooperation in preventing both nuclear accidents and nuclear war. 'The quality of training and retraining of personnel must be raised. Responsibility for the future efficiency and safety of nuclear power plants in operation must be intensified.' "[14] "In calling for a worldwide effort to improve nuclear safety, the report cited the potential problems of large-scale fallout, terrorism, the spread of nuclear weapons and other 'dangers of an international character' that could offset the gains in energy supply. These dangers, the report said, call for 'the fundamental necessity of deep international cooperation.' "[15]

The technical deficiencies in the Chernobyl disaster were of secondary significance compared to this account of the human failure. Because of the earlier Soviet refusal to reveal the causes of the disaster and its scope, Western experts early on devoted much effort to trying to figure out what went wrong and speculated about the extent of the damage. The containment question was an early concern of American experts who suggested that the design of the Soviet nuclear plants did not provide sufficient protection against the possibility of a "melt-through" and escaping radiation. Some felt that the concrete foundations under Soviet reactors were of minimal thickness compared to what was required for U.S. nuclear facilities. A melt-through at Chernobyl would have greatly increased the local radiation damage, contaminating groundwater and threatening, certainly, the water supply of the nearby major city of Kiev. Soviet nuclear experts at the scene labored strenuously and successfully to ensure against a melt-through by tunneling under the Chernobyl reactor and reinforcing its concrete floor.

Western experts were similarly concerned about the aboveground reactor housing. Most Western reactors are enclosed in a sealed concrete and steel shell quite different in design from Soviet nuclear power plants, which lack airtight features. However, a review of plant design, in the aftermath of Chernobyl, indicated that perhaps as many as twenty-four U.S. plants would prove vulnerable to major radiation leakage in the event of a severe reactor accident.[16]

A second technical criticism in the West addressed the possible inadequacy of monitoring and safety devices which automatically shut down the reactor in emergency situations. After the Three Mile Island incident in 1979 a key Soviet spokesman scoffed at the concern in the United States for safety and backup systems. This Soviet expert suggested that the real explanation for this U.S. emphasis on safety systems was the heavy investment by the U.S. power industry in the older fossil fuel technologies.[17] After the details of the Chernobyl accident came to light Soviet concern centered on the ease with which the monitoring and safety devices were ignored or turned off by their Chernobyl operators.

A third technical criticism of the Soviet nuclear power industry centered on the design of the Chernobyl graphite-moderated reactor, "a direct descendant of the world's first nuclear power plant, which went into operation at Obinsk in the Soviet Union in 1954, . . . three years before the first U.S. commercial power plant in Shippingport, Pennsylvania."[18] This type of reactor makes up about half of the fifty Soviet nuclear power reactors. It has the advantage of operating on only modestly enriched uranium 235 and can be refueled without the necessity of shutting down the reactor. Its chief drawback, besides containing "more chemically combustible material than Western reactors," is its instability at certain levels of operation and the ease with which it can be brought "to a 'runaway' condition."[19] One Western expert stated that at the time of the disaster the Chernobyl operators were trying, in effect, "to balance a baseball on top of a watermelon."[20] In the official report Soviet authorities indicated that consideration was being given to modifications in the design of the RBMK graphite-moderated reactor. Two mentioned were "altering the uranium fuel composition to increase reactor stability and lengthening the control rods for faster emergency shutdowns."[21]

One final but major concern fixed upon the location of a number of Soviet nuclear power plants. It was pointed out that the Soviets have "built nuclear facilities within eight miles of cities such as Gorky, Voronezh, Odessa, Kharkov, and Bilibinsk. These plants were designed to provide both electricity and steam for district heating systems. They had to be close to the city centers so that the steam could be distributed without serious losses."[22] The president of the Soviet Academy of Sciences, Anatoly Alexandrov, in the days before Chernobyl, expressed great confidence in Soviet nuclear power technology, remarking on one occasion "that in contrast to Western practice, Soviet nuclear facilities can be built in the middle of residential areas because they are absolutely safe."[23]

The Chernobyl disaster has left a deep, brooding anxiety in many parts of Europe and, no doubt, also in the Soviet Union. The major worldwide response has been an effort to enhance safety through the intensification of operator training and the improvement of communications between nations. The *New York Times* on October 27, 1986, reported that "despite statements soon after the April 26 accident that it involved a reactor design different from Western units, experts are now concluding that Chernobyl in fact has important lessons for all nuclear power plants." Dr. Richard Wilson, a Harvard physicist, commented, "No one concerned with nuclear power, in the United States or elsewhere, can pretend that the Chernobyl accident makes no difference."[24] The efforts at reform center on the human tendency to relax vigilance with increased familiarity with the technology—a tendency that can be countered only by a constant reiteration of the dangers involved in this form of power production. Familiarity cannot be allowed to breed contempt. Thus, just as the U.S. nuclear power industry addressed the need to improve the education and vigilance levels of its operators after Three Mile Island, so now the Soviet Union has taken similar steps. The severity of the Chernobyl accident, however, has alerted people everywhere to the fact that nuclear power must be regarded not only as a *national* resource: it bears responsibility for each nation utilizing it to communicate with all surrounding nations and peoples. As one authority has put it, "No reactor is an island unto itself."[25]

One final observation about the Chernobyl event needs to be mentioned. The specter of nuclear fallout, nuclear radiation, can create a very special fear and dread. Robert Jay Lifton, a professor of psychiatry and psychology at the City University of New York, made an earlier study of the human costs and effects of the bombing of Hiroshima,[26] and, after Chernobyl, offered comment:

> In addition to possible physical danger from radiation, millions of people in the Soviet Union, other parts of Eastern Europe, Scandinavia and elsewhere have been exposed to a lifelong fear of invisible contamination.
> I encountered that fear first in Hiroshima survivors and later in the people exposed to the nuclear accident at Three Mile Island. Deadly harm is threatened not by a visible substance like fire or flood water, from which you can flee to a relatively safe position, but by something far more insidi-

ous. It cannot be detected by senses and may strike at any time. While you speak of invisible contamination from exposure of toxic chemicals, radiation has an added aura of dread associated with limitless danger, fearful mystery and images of Hiroshima and Nagasaki.

Efforts by authorities to control such disaster can, for those exposed, assume qualities of absurdity and deception—beginning with characteristic reassurances of safety, followed by partial reversals and by harried and contradictory evacuation arrangements.[27]

There can be no question that the Chernobyl disaster was a human challenge of major proportion. Heroism on the part of many involved in the event, especially the fire fighters, was clear-cut and notable. The Soviet authorities were fully justified in calling attention to this heroism, but the fear and the strangeness of the danger apparently also caused many to shirk their duties and to flee. On June 16, 1986, the *New York Times* gave account of a Soviet report on the dismissal of the director and chief engineer of the Chernobyl power station.

Pravda said . . . [the two] failed "to insure correct and firm leadership in the difficult conditions of the accident and displayed irresponsibility and inability to organize." Pravda further reported that one plant deputy director . . . fled from his post "at the most difficult moment" and that two other deputy directors . . . "did not fulfill their official duties with proper responsibility." . . . The paper also talked of the urgent need to fill vacancies at the power station caused by the flight of some workers and supervisors. "Because of insufficient organization and educational work with people, a portion of workers from the power station are still 'on the run.' . . . These include foremen of shifts and senior technicians."[28]

This story of human heroism, human failure and cowardice, is a further dimension of the Chernobyl story. It marked in its own way a new human testing, one no longer related to ideology or patriotism but to human survival on a broad new scale.

If one goes some months farther back into the year 1986, into January, and to that other notable technological disaster, Challenger, one is confronted with an event of a different order—but also with some suggestive parallels.

Unlike Chernobyl, the Challenger event was not clouded in mystery. It took place not only in the sky over Cape Canaveral but was viewed on the television sets of literally millions of viewers worldwide. The extent and scope of the disaster was immediately apparent: the death of seven American astronauts, the worst space accident to that point in history. Unlike Chernobyl it did not pose a threat to a major population center or leave residual toxic aftereffects. It was a local accident but one very much bound up with a nation's self-image, and in this regard it shared at least some similarities with the Chernobyl accident. Nations take much pride in their technological achievements and implicitly boast of their expertise. In this case Challenger represented a major setback to U.S. technological prestige, just as Chernobyl had a similar impact for the Soviet Union.

It was, however, the personal tragedy that commanded the first reaction to Challenger. The personal profiles of the seven astronauts had been widely publicized prior to the flight, especially that of Christa McAuliffe, the high school teacher who was to be "the first civilian" in space. Two U.S. congressmen had preceded McAuliffe on earlier space shuttle flights, but McAuliffe had been selected to mark the transition from a military, test-pilot-dominated program to a civilian-oriented one.[29] Because of this strategic shift in focus, special news coverage was devoted to the personal stories of the Challenger crew. They seemed in fact to have been selected for the purpose of projecting a national image, and the democratic nature of the U.S. program: two women, one Jewish and one Irish-Catholic, an Afro-American physicist, a Japanese-American engineer.

In investigating the cause of the accident, the commission appointed by President Reagan on February 4, one week after the accident, quickly centered its attention on the right side booster rocket as likely cause of the accident. In fact, two days before the presidential commission was appointed NASA released photographs of the lift-off which revealed an "unusual plume of smoke" near the base of the right side booster rocket.[30] Subsequent investigations by the commission brought to light the fact that middle-level space agency officials, almost immediately after the accident, had fixed upon faulty O-ring seals in the booster rocket as probable cause of the disaster. This information, however, was not passed on to top NASA management until almost one week later.[31] The commission's subsequent investigation revealed that the O-ring seals had earlier been the subject of concern by engineers, both in NASA and the chief supplier Morton-Thiokol, Inc. Temperature tolerances for the seals had been fixed at 40 to 90 degrees Fahrenheit. Thus Morton-Thiokol's chief engineer at Cape Canaveral at the time of the launch argued against clearance for the flight because of the near-freezing temperatures, but he was overruled by a Morton-Thiokol supervisor at the booster division office in Wasatch, Utah.

The commission's final report, issued on June 10, identified the O-ring seals on the booster rocket as the "simple physical cause" of the disaster but went on to cite management problems in communication and decision-making procedures as a major factor in the final tragedy.[32] NASA management had hoped to move the space shuttle program on to a schedule of one flight every three weeks, and the pressure of these schedules contributed to flawed judgment by top-level officials. The risk factor associated with the Challenger flight—and with previous shuttle launches—was minimized. One senior astronaut expressed anger that he and his fellow astronauts had not been properly informed on these dangers,[33] and Dr. Richard P. Feynman, a world-renowned physicist and member of the President's Commission, declared that NASA's managers had exaggerated the shuttle's reliability "to the point of fantasy."[34] Something of a parallel between the Challenger and Chernobyl disasters exists here in the form of managerial, technical overconfidence. As one editorial put it: "The shuttle is meant to fly routinely into space, but a hazardous routine practiced often enough makes accidents inevitable."[35]

Clearly there is a vast difference, in threat and destruction, between a nuclear power plant accident and a rocket accident. The former has, at least to this point in time, much more wide-ranging consequences, much greater destructive potential. But the lessons of both are virtually the same in demanding of the human agents, at either the operational or the managerial level, rigorous indoctrination and renewed vigilance. A very special kind of education is required. The Soviet report on Chernobyl called for raising "the quality of training and *retraining*."[36] In the context of the machines of power which technology has created, the human community must, as it were, educate itself against itself. In this context we have a tendency to become our own—and our neighbors'—worst enemy. This no doubt is an old truth, but the potential for disaster makes it an ever more pressing truth.

If Challenger and Chernobyl at one point say something similar, there is, I believe, a special nuance in the Challenger event that deserves additional discussion. Here we return to that feature of the Challenger flight which was intended to make it different from all previous shuttle flights: the transition from a military/test-pilot program to an essentially civilian one, open to ordinary citizens. Christa McAuliffe was to be the first "civilian astronaut," the pioneer in a program that would allow people from all walks of life—at least those who could afford it—to take time off from their employment and with four months of special training and conditioning experience the exhilaration of space travel.

However, it is not this program of civilian emphasis which warrants attention so much as the decision to select a teacher as "the first civilian in space." In the summer of 1984 the National Aeronautics and Space Administration recommended to President Reagan a list of professions for this first civilian space flight with top preference being given to an elementary or secondary school teacher. President Reagan concurred in the NASA recommendation; and on August 27, 1984, in the midst of his reelection campaign, he announced the decision to select a teacher for the fateful Challenger flight. The director of NASA at the time, James M. Beggs, said that the recommendation of a teacher was made "because teachers are good communicators, have a life-long effect on their students and can inspire young people to become interested in space, science and mathematics. . . . 'This agency,' [he declared,] 'lives and dies by whether we can attract top talent and keep the kids interested in the program.' "[37]

One must note the political importance of this announcement in the middle of a presidential campaign, when both Republican and Democratic parties were vying for the support of the powerful teachers unions. But there is another context in which the decision must be understood and interpreted, one underlined by the quote from NASA's James Beggs: "This agency lives and dies by whether we can attract top talent and keep the kids interested in the program."

In late April of 1983 a bipartisan federal commission, appointed two years earlier by Secretary of Education T. H. Bell, reported that "the educational foundations of our society are presently being eroded by a rising tide of mediocrity that threatens our very future as a Nation and as a people. What was unimaginable a generation ago has begun to occur—others are matching and surpassing our educational attainments."[38] This report gained widespread attention across the nation, and was followed soon afterward, on May 4, by a second major educational report sponsored by the Educational Commission of the States— a national body representing officials from state government and public education. This second report, the work of a special task force of "forty-one governors, corporate leaders, and other prominent figures, asserted that the poor quality of American public schools was threatening the military, economic and social well-being of the country. . . . 'Our schools are not doing an adequate job of educating for today's requirements in the workplace much less tomorrow's.' "[39]

The chief feature of both these reports, the federal government's *A Nation at Risk* and the *Report of the National Task Force on Education for Economic Growth,* was the charge that the United States' public education system was at fault for the decline of the nation's technological-economic leadership vis-à-vis other leading industrial nations. In *A Nation at Risk* the imagery used in the second paragraph of the report is one of warfare: "If an unfriendly foreign power had attempted to impose on America the mediocre educational performance that exists today we might well have viewed it as an act of war."[40] The peculiar use of this imagery in such a context heightened the sense of crisis and led to the identification of a national threat, one to which the American educational system was called to respond. It was, however, no longer the Soviet Union, which demanded the "technological reform" of American education—as had occurred earlier with the launching of Sputnik in 1957. Now the enemy was declared to be Japan and West Germany, two erstwhile political allies, which the report clearly identified as technological-economic foes.

With all the ferment generated by these critical reports, it was inevitable that NASA would recommend selection of a teacher as the first civilian in space and that the President of the United States would concur in this recommendation. Just as the NASA director, Beggs, saw the survival of his own agency as requiring the enlistment of elementary and secondary education for the goals and purposes of the space program, so also President Reagan offered comment: "When that shuttle lifts off—all America will be reminded of the crucial role teachers and education play in the life of our nation. I can't think of a better lesson for our children, and our country."[41] Ten days after the disaster, President Reagan reaffirmed his commitment to send a teacher into space as a means of underscoring "the Administration's commitment to technology and education."[42]

At the state level the drive to reform public education which followed these national studies has been led by various groups, most often by business groups that have felt the competition of Japanese and German technology in the commercial and trade field. Sometimes it has been pushed by the governors who have seen the well-being of their states in jeopardy. The initiative and pattern of reform naturally varies from state to state, but almost all states and local communities have felt the new pressures for educational change.

Minnesota, my home state, can be used as an example of how technology has come to play a lead role in the reform of the educational enterprise. Minnesota has had one of the better public education systems in the nation—at least by pre-1983 standards. In 1985 it led the fifty states in the percentage of its young people who completed high school (90 percent) and it ranked third among the states in one of the major college entrance tests (the ACT). The percentage of its young people who go on to college, about 57 percent, is also among the nation's highest. It has a strong system of public higher education, with an impressive cadre of high-quality private colleges to complement the state university system.

In 1984, however, a group called the Minnesota Business Partnership, representing virtually all the major corporations in the state, funded a study of Minnesota public education, hiring a California education consulting firm to do the study.[43] In its final report, the consulting firm devoted special attention to attacking the sense of pride and well-being which the Minnesota citizenry had come to place in its educational system,[44] and then went on to identify deficiencies in critical thinking and problem solving skills. The report declared: "Doing better is more than a desirable goal: it may be a necessity for future high school graduates. Employment opportunities are likely to be greatly influenced by global competition and the influx of new technologies into the workplace. Minnesota's continued economic prosperity will require highly skilled managers, scientists, and technical experts."[45] The major recommendation of the consulting firm, besides increased standard testing at designated grade levels, was a modified form of the voucher system, a structural reform that abandons the principle of the neighborhood or district school in favor of parental selection of schools of choice. In this restructuring, state funds follow the pupils to the school of choice, though in the consultant's report it was suggested that this option should be limited to the eleventh and twelfth grades. This proposal was taken up and adapted by Minnesota's Democratic-Farmer-Labor governor, Rudy Perpich, who made it the substance of his own reform program, publicized under the slogans "Open Enrollment" and "Access to Excellence." Along with the assurance of parental and student choice of schools the reform program implicitly delegated to the schools the power to control admissions. In this program competition among the public schools was projected as the chief means of upgrading public education.

This plan met with important opposition as it was originally presented by the governor and the governor-appointed Commissioner of Education. The teachers unions and the economically hard-pressed rural, farming, and mining communities of the state argued against the proposal on the basis of a likely loss of teacher jobs, the closing of a number of rural schools, and the siphoning off of the better students from area schools. This original opposition was strong enough to force the governor, in his reelection campaign of 1986, to promise *not* to press his educational reform measure until the teachers unions and the local school boards had a chance to provide more input into the reform proposal.[46]

No small feature of the governor's original proposal was the establishment of specialized residential high schools in science, technology, and math, along with similar schools in the fine arts and the humanities. This accent upon specialization is clearly designed to respond to the demands of the business community for a skilled labor pool, attuned to the growing demand of technological competition. The same program has been initiated at the university level where a restructuring program called "Commitment to Focus" projects a 25 percent reduction in undergraduate liberal arts enrollment[47] as a step to furthering the university's function as a research institution, again with heavy emphasis upon the science and technology divisions. Along with "Commitment to Focus" the State of Minnesota is committed to providing long-term support to the development of a high-technology center which Governor Perpich regarded as essential to his oft-stated purpose of establishing Minnesota as "the brain-power state."

There can be little question that the real driving force of this national educational reform movement is the growing impact of technology upon the competitive relationship of nations and states. The large multinational corporations, in their struggle to maintain and expand their command of markets, are the agents of this competitive drive. Thus technology represents a potential threat to survival not only in such areas as nuclear war, and/or nuclear power accidents, but also in the day-to-day worldwide competitive struggle of the corporate giants. In this sphere technology is perceived as the means to power—and survival—within the world market economy. It serves, ambiguously, as the major source of both security and insecurity in our contemporary world. Education is called to the forefront to guard against society's hurt by technology but above all to assure technology's growth.

Here the perspective of history is helpful in furthering our understanding of what is happening in the present situation. Carl Becker's insistence on seeing things in sequence lends warrant for this historical excursus. In the third and fourth decades of the last century, the young American republic began a process of stocktaking, a reexamination of goals and purposes. It was a critical period in the national history and also in the history of education in America. It was the time of the common school and the founding of state systems of education. These were affirmed as essential to the continued development of the nation and its people. The times were troubled; new forces were at work in society. Many of the ideals of the American Revolution and the Declaration of Independence were felt to be unrealized. A widespread fear of anarchy was common, triggered by domestic unrest and the failure of the French Revolution. The first impact of the Industrial Revolution was just beginning to be felt. It was in this context that Horace Mann emerged as the influential advocate of a tax-supported system of common, public education and of normal schools for the training of teachers. In a major work on the history of American education,[48] Lawrence A. Cremin has described the vision underlying Mann's achievement. Certainly many before him had asserted the necessity and hope of education in the republic: Thomas Jefferson, George Washington, Benjamin Rush, James Madison, to name only a few.[49] But it was Mann who worked to give form and substance to this hope. Already accomplished as lawyer, state legislator, and senator in Massachusetts, Mann was appointed the first secretary of the newly established state board of education in 1837. With virtually no political power, he began to preach the cause of state-supported education throughout Massachusetts and was eventually able to ensure a more uniform, effective schooling in knowledge and citizenship. It is the latter point that is of special note. Cremin writes:

> Mann's ideal common school enbodied all the elements he deemed essential to education in a republic. It would be common, not as a school for common people—but rather as a school common to all people. It would be open to all and supported by tax funds. It would be for rich and poor alike, the equal of any private institution. And, by receiving children of all creeds, classes, and backgrounds . . . it would kindle a spirit of unity and mutual respect that the conflicts of adult life could never destroy. . . . He saw social harmony as a prime goal of popular education.[50]

Mann himself offered these words:

> In a government like ours, each individual must think of the welfare of the state as well as of the welfare of his own family, and therefore, of the children of others as well as of his own. It becomes then, a momentous question, whether the children in our schools are educated in reference to themselves and their private interests only, or with a regard to the great social duties and prerogatives that await them in [adulthood] for, however loftily the intellect of man may have been gifted, however skillfully it may have been trained, if it be not guided by a sense of justice, a love of mankind and a devotion to duty, its possessor is only a more splendid, as he is a more dangerous barbarian.[51]

On the grounds of the Massachusetts state capitol building in Boston are found the statues of two figures: Daniel Webster and Horace Mann.[52] The two represent a profound statement of what counted in another age: politics and education, education and politics. The two stood together and represented the substance of hope. How has it come about that the political hope has waned and that now education is asked to serve technology and the well-being, in the first instance, of business enterprise in its competition at home and abroad? How is it that the common school and the goal of participation in the political process no longer serve as "our" major purpose?

There is an important difference between two definitions of progress that have emerged from this discussion, two definitions implied in the question Has technology become our history? In one, the technological view of progress, reliance is placed upon a technical elite to move humanity forward. The costs of such progress tend to be hidden in governmental budgets, in the power and mechanics of corporate decision-making, in the supposed benignity of human invention. In this view the order of nature is made to bear the chief cost of progress and human society is spared the pain of conscious sacrifice, but within this view a troubling unease is stirring. The goal of such progress is never clearly stated—power, novelty, human comfort, sensory enhancement? Then events like Challenger and Chernobyl intervene and the sense spreads that no one really is in control and that we all, all humanity, may be drifting toward disaster—climactic or gradual, but disaster. The sense spreads that death, after all, still haunts the human enterprise. This death, however, is one of our own making.

The other view of progress, suggested in the brief backward look at Horace Mann and the purposes of American public education in the early decades of the nineteenth century, defines progress in terms of citizenship and the shaping of a cohesive, fulfilling, human society. Here the costs of meaningful life are consciously borne by the citizenry in the common project of community building. The conquest of nature is not the goal, rather the elimination of disruptive, alienating, divisive forces within society itself. In this view social duties are given primary focus and the costs are more clearly defined. In this second but earlier view of progress, we ourselves are the ones who bear the cost. The sacrifice is our own, not nature's.

In the next two chapters we shall offer an interpretation of how the historic shift to a technological view of progress has come about, how we find ourselves in our present situation.

2

TECHNOLOGY AND THE
IDEA OF PROGRESS

As suggested in chapter 1, a review of the history of education in America points up the deep commitment to the political ideas of the American republic which underlay the establishment of the public school system. Earlier, in the colonial period, much of the initiative for the schooling of the young came from the religious community, but with the success of the American Revolution the social bonds became more political than religious. This is not to say that the increasingly fractured religious communities did not play a role in the public education movement. They did, and the Bible continued to be widely used as a text for instruction in reading and morals.[1] It was, however, chiefly the history of the successful struggle for American independence and the commitment to the ideals of that struggle which inspired the educational reforms of the first half of the nineteenth century. Again Horace Mann offers us a statement of the depth of that commitment. "Revolutions which change only the surface of society can be effected in a day," Mann wrote, "but revolutions working down among the primordial elements of human character . . . cannot be accomplished by one convulsive effort, though every fibre in the nation should be strained in the endeavor."[2] In Mann's view, it was the slow, plodding work of teachers and pupils in the common schools which was to secure and fulfill the revolution.

This was a very sober but certainly deeply felt affirmation of the belief in Progress, a seventeenth- and eighteenth-century idea which dominated the thought of the European Enlightenment and which was shared by many of the Founding Fathers in the Declaration of Independence and in the Constitution as well. To be sure, the Revolution was immediately concerned with throwing off the British yoke, and many believed that this was the sole goal, but others saw and interpreted what was happening in broader terms, intended to give hope to all humanity. The motto on the reverse of the Great Seal of the United States, "Novus Ordo Seclorum," a "new order of the ages," gives expression to this faith. The framers of the Constitution, despite the bias of class and property which also played an important part in their work,[3] saw the need of carefully crafting a structure of government that balanced private and sectional interest with the well-being and possibilities for growth of the commonwealth. Horace Mann affirmed the political advances but believed also in the need of moral education in the schools to bring the republic to full flower. Education in reading and writing was not enough. A "revolution in character" was essential to the progress of the nation.[4]

This hope and expectation of social progress was little related to the state of technology at the time. The development of machine technology in America, especially in relation to the development of the textile industry in New England in the 1820s, was viewed less as an ally than as a threat. In a provocative study of the relationship of technology to the values of the American republic, John F. Kasson has given account of the assimilation of technology by the young nation. In charting this history Kasson gives numerous examples of the early embrace of technology, its necessity in the War of Independence, then the enthusiasm that attended the advances of textile mill, railroad, and steamboat.[5] The title of Kasson's work states the problem: "Civilizing the Machine." The steam engine in its many applications was dramatic and even awe-inspiring, but in England it had contributed to a factory system that was humanly degrading. The question posed for the young American nation was whether the new technology could be assimilated without threatening the growth in social harmony which was looked to as a national goal. Reporting upon this history, Kasson concludes that at the end of the nineteenth century "republicanism" no longer possessed "the centrality and coherence that made it, from the Revolution through the nineteenth century, such an important shaping ideology in Americans' response to technology. Instead, new political strategies and categories of value . . . [had] to be formulated to address the enduring and elusive problem of civilizing the machine."[6]

Kasson infers—as we also have suggested—that technology has moved out beyond, away from, the earlier vision of purposive history. Though the image is not his, Kasson's argument suggests that the most frequented museum in the world, the Smithsonian Institution's Air and Space Museum in Washington, D.C., has become the real symbol of progress in our time and that the values enshrined elsewhere in Washington, in the monuments to Washington, to Jefferson, to Lincoln, no longer suffice to guide and direct what history is becoming. It is in the space museum in Washington that one encounters the enthusiasm, the excitement of the young. To be sure, loyalty to the ideals of the American republic, the sense of national identity, are affirmed at the older shrines. But it is the adventure of space,[7] the capitalistic commitment to technological innovation and profit, the simple fascination with the new, which have superseded, if they have not subtly subverted the goal of a humane, social harmony. It is technology that has come to provide the meaning of the term "Progress."

Technology did not give rise to the idea of Progress any more than it established the American republic. It certainly helped to broaden support for the idea by providing an abundance of material goods in the nineteenth century, but the formulation of the idea itself was another matter. It is important to consider the origin and development of the idea of Progress in order to understand better where American society currently stands in relation to it.

It is a surprising fact that a systematic study of the origins of the idea of Progress was not seriously undertaken by the intellectual community until 1920.[8] At that time the Cambridge historian J. B. Bury published his pioneering work entitled simply *The Idea of Progress*. In this work Bury makes the point that the belief in Progress is a distinctively modern idea, coming to the fore in the seventeenth and eighteenth centuries as a major tenet of the European Enlightenment and then dominating the ethos of the nineteenth century and on into the twentieth century. He describes the idea in the following terms:

> [This] idea of human Progress is a theory which involves a synthesis of the past and a prophecy of the future. It is based on an interpretation of history which regards men as slowly advancing . . . in a definite and desirable direction, and infers that this progress will continue indefinitely. . . . It implies that . . . a condition of general happiness will ultimately be enjoyed, which will justify the whole process of civilization. . . . The process must be the necessary outcome of the psychical and social nature of man; it must not be at the mercy of an external will; otherwise there would be no guarantee of its continuance and its issue.[9]

The French philosopher Auguste Comte and the English historian Walter Bagehot had earlier asserted that Progress, as a definition of human meaning, was unknown to the world of Greece and Rome. Bury goes on in his ground-breaking work to offer explanation why this was so, why the Greco-Roman world did not formulate such an idea even though some of its great minds were well aware of periodic cultural and technological advances. For one thing he suggests that the recorded history of the Greeks was not of sufficient length to establish a pattern of long-term improvement. The various technical advances were understood not as an outgrowth of the science of the time, but rather as haphazard innovations, without enduring promise.

In addition, the general assumption of a "Golden Age" of the past worked against an expectation of Progress. The Golden Age was believed to have been a period of simplicity but also of universal human satisfaction. This was subsequently marred by a "fall"; and since that time, life had followed a course of general degradation, interrupted by occasional movements of cultural advance. Bury argues that this concept of the Golden Age stood as a major obstacle to any idea of progressive improvement in the human condition; that it served as a kind of backdrop to the idea of recurring cycles. With nature as a model, the Pythagoreans and the Stoics declared that history followed a pattern of endless cycles. And even though Seneca, a later Stoic, proclaimed the likelihood of a long-term advance in knowledge, he and other Stoics did not regard such advances as an improvement in the general human condition. Humanity, it was believed, was doomed to persistent corruption and thus an increase of knowledge was consolation only for a few.

Bury contends that not only the belief in recurring cycles but also the belief in *moira*, translated most frequently as "fate," militated against a belief in Progress. Moira represented a fixed order of things beyond the control of either men or gods. It defined functions and set limits. Moira called for human resignation, not resistance or revision. To defy fate was, in effect, to self-destruct. Again, here was an ethos, a view of reality, which did not allow for Progress.

In general the Greek mind conceived of change in negative terms. For the Greeks the major attraction of philosophical thought was its promise of rising above change and offering description of an enduring reality. The "essence" of a thing was that rationally defined characteristic which made a group of things distinctive, and was capable of overcoming the "accidental" features of particular members of the group. To move from the many to the one, from the particular to the general in rational thought was to move in the direction of greater reality and away from the world of change and decay. Matter was viewed as refractory, making for the distortion of ideas or forms. Thus to contemplate the "pure form" of things was to achieve the highest purpose of the mind. Clearly, such an ethos, such an intellectual outlook, did not lend itself to progressive modes of thought; rather it represented an effort to escape from the world of change. Change was viewed as the enemy, not a basis for hope.[10]

With the spread of Christianity into the Greco-Roman world, there was considerable assimilation of these Greek ideas into the theology of the church, but Bury notes two points in Christian thought which offered opposition to the previous pattern of Greek thought. This opposition, Bury suggests, represents a movement in the direction of the later belief in Progress. He observes that in Judeo-Christian thought

> the history of the earth was recognised as a unique phenomenon in time; it would never occur again, or anything resembling it. More important than all is the fact that Christian theology constructed a synthesis which for the first time attempted to give a definite meaning to the whole course of human events, a synthesis which represents the past as leading up to a definite and desirable goal in the future. Once this belief had been generally adopted and prevailed for centuries men might discard it along with the doctrine of Providence on which it rested, but they could not be content to return again to such views as satisfied the ancients, for whom human history, apprehended as a whole, was a tale of little meaning.[11]

Bury points out that along with this linear concept of history, Christianity helped to establish the idea of the ecumene, the inhabited world, the totality of the human race, as the arena of meaning, not some restricted part, not the city or polis, as in Greek thought. The idea of the ecumene was not unique to Christianity since it found expression in the conquests of Alexander, in Stoic doctrine, and in the political achievements of the Roman Empire; but Christianity certainly maintained and helped propagate the idea in the form of the universal church.[12]

Bury goes on to say that though Christianity helped overcome some of the conceptual barriers to the belief in Progress, it nonetheless posed an obstacle to that belief at two points, first in its otherworldliness and second in its concept of Providence, the belief that a divine agency, not a human one, was the controlling force in history.

Such was largely the situation through the Middle Ages to the seventeenth century. But with the Italian Renaissance and its spread into northern Europe, Bury contends that a new and positive appraisal of life in this world came increasingly to oppose medieval otherworldliness and the emphasis upon a sinful, fallen humanity. A new enthusiasm for learning was stirred by the recovery and circulation of ancient Greek and Roman texts, an ambiguous development since it reinforced the veneration of the past. Bury observes that "most active minds were engaged in rediscovering, elaborating, criticising and imitating what was old."[13] Thus the Renaissance too failed a belief in Progress.

In the remainder of his discussion Bury devotes himself to describing the various steps, the contributions of particular thinkers, which produced the idea of Progress. The highlight of this development was the sixteenth-century Copernican Revolution, the substitution of a sun-centered for an earth-centered cosmos, a step that freed up the Western mind from enslavement to past authorities and helped center attention on expanding vistas of knowledge extending into the future. This shift in vision Bury traces in the late sixteenth-century works of the French historian Jean Bodin (1530–1596), the classical scholar Louis LeRoy (sixteenth century), the English philosopher and Lord Chancellor Francis Bacon (1561–1626), and the especially important seventeenth-century mathematician and philosopher René Descartes (1596–1650). In these men Bury charts the spread of the new spirit of inquiry into ever-wider fields of knowledge. In Bacon knowledge becomes the servant of human needs, and in Descartes the belief in Providence was set aside in favor of the universality and uniformity of the laws of nature, a development vital to the continued growth of a sure body of knowledge.

Offering summary of these developments Fontenelle (1657–1757), in the latter half of the seventeenth century, declared that "the sound views of intellectual men in successive generations will continually add up" and that this growth in knowledge was independent of "an unpredictable external will."[14] Fontenelle's widely published work *Conversations on the Plurality of Worlds* was responsible for greatly expanding awareness of the new scientific view of the universe. This book was almost immediately translated into English and other languages and introduced the growing reading public to the new worldview with all of its ramifications.

Lacking, however, in Fontenelle's work was any sense for the improvement of social and political life. His interest lay solely in the spread of the new learning, with little or no regard for its application to daily life. It was the Abbé de Saint-Pierre (1658–1743) who provided this latter vision. A wellspring of "rational" projects of all sorts, in government, in finance, in education, the Abbé de Saint-Pierre believed that the reasonableness of his varied proposals would be sufficient to assure their adoption. In this he was disappointed, but he *did* succeed in disseminating the thought and the hope that government and laws could help to reshape for the good the lives of the general populace, that knowledge should serve this purpose, and that human reason was the sure means to universal human Progress.[15]

Though himself no believer in Progress, the French philosopher Montesquieu (1689–1755) argued that social phenomena, no less than natural, were subject to laws and rational analysis. Voltaire (1694–1778), a doubt-full and cynical believer in Progress, argued in his *Essay on the Manners and Mind of Nations* that wars, superstition, and religions were the chief obstacles to human progress. Voltaire denied that there was any divine order to history and argued that reason alone bore the hope of human betterment.

In the thirty or forty years prior to the French Revolution, the French Encyclopedists added still another element to the emerging belief in Progress by declaring a faith in the perfectibility of humankind. Bury remarks that the contributors to the great eighteenth-century compendium of the new learning, "carried on the campaign against authority and superstition. . . . It was the work of men who . . . had ideals, positive purposes, and social hopes. They were not only confident in reason and in science, but most of them had also a more or less definite belief in the possibility of an advance of humanity towards perfection."[16] Convinced of the malleability of humankind, both intellectually and morally, they looked to education and the reform of social institutions as the means of guiding humanity to a better future. Past differences between peoples, due to varied education and social circumstances, could be overcome and all peoples would eventually enjoy a fulfilling future human society.

Bury notes that some of the contributors to the *Encyclopedia* were especially concerned with economic theory and defined the goal of human happiness in materialistic terms. Called Physiocrats, they "assumed as their first principle the eudaemonic value of civilisation, declared that temporal happiness is attainable, and threw all their weight into the scales against the doctrine of [civilization's regress]." Bury says of the Physiocrats: "By liberty the Economists meant economic liberty. Neither they nor the Philosophers nor Rousseau, the father of modern democracy, had any just conception of what political liberty means. . . . They never challenged the principle of a despotic government, they only contended that the despotism must be enlightened."[17] The great Scottish economist Adam Smith shared many of these views and helped reinforce the idea that the future held promise of "an indefinite augmentation of wealth and well-being." Opulence was regarded as a fundamental guarantor of civilization and "the happiness of mankind."[18]

Continuing his description of the development of the idea of Progress, Bury ascribes to Condorcet (1743–1794) credit for the thought that the increase of knowledge assures and underlies social progress. In Condorcet's words "the history of civilisation is the history of enlightenment." Condorcet divided history into ten periods which were marked off chiefly on the basis of advances in knowledge and certain steps in the technology of knowledge (e.g., the alphabet and the printing press). He believed that once this direction of history was established humankind could "accelerate the rate of progression."[19] Here Bury comments:

The significance [of Condorcet's final work, *Sketch of a Historical Picture of the Progress of the Human Mind*] lies in this, that towards the close of an intellectual movement [the Enlightenment] it concentrated attention on the most important, though hitherto not the most prominent, ideal which that movement had disseminated, and, as it were, officially announced human Progress as the leading problem that claimed the interest of mankind.[20]

The French Revolution posed something of a setback to the belief in Progress since it tended to highlight the irrationality that continued to plague humanity. The Revolution's failure led many to work for a restoration of the old order. There followed, in France and some other countries, a resurgence of conservative Catholic thought. But Saint-Simon (1760–1825) and especially Auguste Comte (1798–1857) reaffirmed the progressive point of view by identifying a "law of progress" which underlay the turbulence of surface events. Comte maintained that there were three stages in the forward march of history: the theological, the metaphysical, and the positivist-scientific. These three historical stages corresponded also to a kind of developmental psychology believed to be traceable not only in the individual but in the growth of the various fields of science. In the first stage, "the mind invents" (belief in imaginary deities); in the second, "it abstracts" (the definition of essences); and in the third stage, "it submits itself to positive facts" (scientific method: observations and experiment). Comte argued that only in his own time, with *his* work, had history come to a scientific inquiry into social phenomena, the practice of "sociology," chief of all the sciences. If at times the growth of these sciences was uneven, if theological and metaphysical elements persisted alongside of various forms of "positive" awareness, this only reflected the intricate, organic relationships within society. Comte maintained that history was moving inevitably and progressively forward.

> The movement of history is due to the deeply rooted though complex instinct which pushes man to ameliorate his condition incessantly, to develop in all ways the sum of his physical, moral, and intellectual life. And all the phenomena of his social life are closely cohesive. . . . By virtue of this cohesion, political, moral, and intellectual progress are inseparable from material progress, and so we find that the phases of his material development correspond to intellectual changes.[21]

Bury asserts that though Comte failed to convince subsequent generations that he had defined the laws of history, he, "more than any preceding thinker [helped] to establish the idea of Progress as a luminary which could not escape men's vision. . . . The massive system wrought out by Comte's speculative genius—his organic scheme of human knowledge, his elaborate analysis of history, his new science of sociology—was a great fact with which European thought was forced to reckon. The soul of this system was Progress."[22]

In written discussion of nineteenth-century developments in the idea of Progress, Bury pays special heed to the increasing role of technology and industrialization in the spread of the idea. At the great Exhibition of London in 1851 tribute was paid to the remarkable strides that had been made in machine technology. The steam engine had revolutionized not only the textile and mining industries but transportation as well. The railroad was viewed as nothing short of a marvel and was hailed in poetry and art. The Prince Consort, who promoted the Exhibition, declared in an official speech: "Gentlemen, the Exhibition of 1851 is to give us a true test and a living picture of the point of development at which the whole of mankind has arrived . . . and a new starting-point from which all nations will be able to direct their future exertions."[23] And Bury then adds:

> Since the Exhibition, western civilisation has advanced steadily, and in some respects more rapidly than any sober mind could have predicted—civilisation, at least, in the conventional sense has been not badly defined as "the development of material ease, of education, of equality, and of aspirations to rise and succeed in life." The most striking advance has been in the technical conveniences of life—that is, in the control over natural forces. It would be superfluous to enumerate the discoveries and inventions since 1850 which have abridged space, economised time, eased bodily suffering, and reduced in some ways the friction of life, though they have increased it in others. This uninterrupted series of technical inventions, proceeding concurrently with immense enlargements of all branches of knowledge, has gradually accustomed the least speculative mind to the conception that civilisation is naturally progressive, and that continuous improvement is part of the order of things.[24]

It is with this accolade to technological progress that Bury's analysis comes to its climax, but he goes on to affirm once again the social dimension of Progress in assessing the impact of Darwin's theory of evolution upon nineteenth-century thought. Bury suggests that with elimination of the idea of the fixity of the species Darwin's theory established developmentalism and transformism as reigning concepts. Though technically "a neutral, scientific conception," Bury argues that evolution became a persuasive support for the belief in Progress when supplemented with the two suppositions that social life obeyed "the same general laws of evolution as nature" and that the process of social evolution involved "an increase of happiness."[25] These social evolutionary ideas found a powerful exponent in the person of Herbert Spencer (1820–1903). Humankind, Spencer asserted, was not possessed of a fixed nature but like nature itself was ever expressing new "development." "Humanity is indefinitely variable, perfectibility is possible."[26] Evil was not a permanent necessity, merely humankind's inadequate adjustment to changing circumstances.

In an assessment of this concluding phase of his study Bury makes the judgment that neither Comte nor Spencer was able to establish Progress as a "scientific hypothesis," as the fixed law of society. He goes on to argue that belief in Progress has become the great dogma of modern society and that it is this belief which lends coherence and unity to Western culture. Progress, Bury asserts, stands as "an important ethical principle" in which "the centre of interest is transferred to the life of future generations who are to enjoy conditions of happiness denied to us, but which our labours and sufferings are to help to bring about."[27]

In a final review and summary Bury writes:

> Looking back on the course of the inquiry, we note how the history of the idea [of Progress] has been connected with the growth of rationalism, and with the struggle for political and religious liberty. The precursors (Bodin and Bacon) lived at a time when the world was consciously emancipating itself from the authority of tradition. . . . The idea took definite shape in France when the old scheme of the universe had been shattered by the victory of the new astronomy and the prestige of Providence . . . was paling before the majesty of the immutable laws of nature. There began a slow but steady reinstatement of the kingdom of this world. The otherworldly dreams of theologians . . . which had ruled so long lost their power and men's earthly home again insinuated itself into their affections, but with the new hope of its becoming a place fit for reasonable beings to live in. We have seen how the belief that our race is travelling towards earthly happiness was propagated by eminent thinkers . . . and all these high-priests and incense-bearers to whom the creed owes its success were rationalists.[28]

Over the years Bury's study of the emergence of the idea of Progress has stood up exceedingly well. Never without some criticism,[29] it nevertheless provided essential clarification of the idea itself and seemed to coalesce with the Western mind's own self-understanding. Especially prominent in Bury's analysis is the juxtaposition of the belief in Progress to the theological concept of divine Providence. Though he allows for popular confusion on this point and also for efforts at "synthesis," Bury asserts that "the fundamental assumptions" of Progress and Providence are "incongruous."[30] And he helps thereby to outline a fundamental shift from a theocentric to an anthropocentric worldview, the transition from a previous reliance upon divine grace to a hope centered in a humanly engineered salvation. Bury's treatment heightens awareness of this historical shift in values and facilitates an understanding of the process of secularization which has increasingly gripped Western culture since the eighteenth century.[31]

In the 1950s Bury's analysis was still very much the dominant work in the field. The Scottish theologian John Baillie wrote in 1951 to correct Bury's too brief notation of Christianity's contribution to the rise of the belief in Progress, accenting the Christian eschatological and millennialist expectation of historical fulfillment. Baillie's book *The Belief in Progress* also properly notes and corrects Bury's inexplicable neglect of the thought of Karl Marx, certainly a very major expression of the nineteenth- and twentieth-century belief in Progress. Baillie's praise of Bury's work, however, was typical of the regard in which it was held. Baillie writes:

> The story of the gradual emergence of this belief from the end of the seventeenth century onwards, and of its development throughout the eighteenth and nineteenth centuries, has been admirably told for us by Bury. . . . Bury indeed has done his work so well that it would be lost labour to attempt here to retraverse with any particularity the ground he covered.[32]

And three years later the Yale intellectual historian Franklin Le Van Baumer comments: "J. B. Bury's *Idea of Progress* is still the standard book on the subject."[33]

It was not until 1980 with the publication of Robert Nisbet's *History of the Idea of Progress* that an effort was made to revise and correct Bury in a major way. In this recent work Nisbet adopts a radically different position from Bury by arguing for the antiquity of the idea of Progress. Drawing especially upon the earlier 1967 work of Ludwig Edelstein, *The Idea of Progress in Classical Antiquity*, Nisbet argues that the idea of Progress was widespread in the Greco-Roman world. Nisbet writes:

> Through the specialized scholarship of such eminent classicists as Ludwig Edelstein, M. I. Finley, W. K. C. Guthrie, and Eric R. Dodds—we have come to see that the Greeks and Romans, contrary to conventional interpretation, *did* have a distinct awareness of a long past, *did* see a measured progression of the arts and sciences and of man's estate on earth, and *did* on occasion refer to a future in which civilization would have gone well beyond what it was in their own time.[34]

But it is primarily the work of Edelstein that inspired Nisbet's brave revision of the history. Nisbet himself offers little original research to establish the viability of his interpretation. Much of what he offers expands on fragments of material which, though they can be readily understood within a cyclical pattern of historical meaning, he chooses to read as examples of the eighteenth-century concept of an inclusive movement of moral, social, and material advance.

For example, Nisbet elaborates on a point made by Edelstein concerning Thucydides' description of cultural advance among the Greeks.[35] However, he fails to note, as does also Edelstein, that Thucydides is primarily concerned to tell the story of Athens' rise to greatness, not the Greeks per se, or humanity in general. Thucydides believed a story is worth telling only if the protagonist, in this case Athens, had achieved greatness. Thucydides' history of the Peloponnesian War is actually set within the framework of a "tragic" reading of history, not a progressive one.

It is ironic that Nisbet cites the name of M. I. Finley among his "eminent" supporting authorities, for Finley is hardly a supporter of the case which Nisbet tries to make. In fact, in 1968, Finley offered a brief but highly critical review of Edelstein's work. After suggesting that one of the great problems for historians is that of distinguishing between sympathy and identification in the treatment of a given subject matter, Finley warns: "Sympathy easily slides into identification, so that a past culture or society begins to look and sound like the historian's image of his own. Sympathy in that disguise requires the people who are the subject of the inquiry to have thought and felt in the right advanced ways." Finley then goes on to charge that Edelstein's argument for essential identity between the ancient and modern idea of progress bears the character of a "confidence trick" in "confusing progress in certain branches of knowledge (but not all)—geometry, astronomy, physics, music, less certainly philosophy—with what we mean by the idea of progress."[36]

Two other features of Nisbet's argument deserve mention. The first is the large role accorded Christian millennialist thought in the development of the idea of Progress. Nisbet's argument here raises questions because in Bury's view the Christian contribution lay chiefly in the rejection of the cyclical view of history; whereas in Nisbet's reading the Greco-Roman cyclical view was much less significant than has been supposed. Nisbet suggests that the Christian "millennialist" contribution lay in its espousal of the "unity of all mankind"—a point Bury also makes—but Nisbet then goes on to list among millennialist contributions the belief in "historical necessity," "the image of progress as the unfolding through long ages of a design present from the very beginning of man's history and far from least, a confidence in the future that would become steadily greater and also more *this* worldly in orientation as compared with *next* worldly." Nisbet then concludes, "To these attributes one other must be added: the emphasis upon the gradual, cumulative, spiritual perfection of mankind, an immanent process that would in time culminate in a golden age of happiness on earth, a millennium with the returned Christ as ruler."[37]

In the light of Nisbet's concluding embrace of the thought of Pierre Teilhard de Chardin, an advocate of the idea of cosmic evolution, the coalescence of religion and science, Marxism and liberal humanism,[38] it is difficult to avoid the conclusion that Nisbet has allowed his philosophical commitments to dictate his historical assessments. Finley's previously quoted complaint about the work of Edelstein appears to apply equally well to Nisbet: "Sympathy easily slides into identification, so that a past culture or society begins to look and sound like the historian's image of his own."

A second aspect of Nisbet's proffered revision of the history of the idea of Progress deserves note. This is his treatment of the fourteenth- to sixteenth-century Renaissance. Once again Nisbet emerges as an innovator, at the opposite end of the spectrum from Bury. For Bury the Renaissance was the expression of a new self-confidence on the part of Western thinkers, a new this-worldliness, a new love of learning even though expressed in a reverence for the past. For Nisbet, however, the Renaissance is chiefly of note for its advocacy of a divisive individualism, one that works against Nisbet's vision of organismic, social advance. Nisbet deplores the subjectivist, narcissistic tendencies he finds in mainstream Renaissance thought. Such "solipsistic" accents, he claims, are destructive of the belief in Progress. And he counters, once again, with his own view of the matter.

> Fundamental to the idea of progress, as we have seen in the . . . preceding chapters, and shall see in all chapters that follow this one, is the premise of historical continuity. . . . Respect for and acceptance of the past is absolutely vital to the theory of progress; without a past, conceived as coming down in cultural substance as well as in time to the present, no principles of development, no stages emerging from one another, and no linear projection to the future are possible.[39]

Because Nisbet interprets the Renaissance, in its major representatives, as rejecting the Middle Ages in favor of the newly recovered learning of Greece and Rome, and thus as rejecting the principle of continuity, he declares that no idea of Progress could exist, much less flourish, in the Renaissance context.

Bury would have agreed with Nisbet that no idea of Progress could emerge in the context of an undue reverence for the past, but Bury saw in the Renaissance, as Nisbet does not, a new affirmation of the meaning of life in *this* world and a new confidence in human abilities and virtues.

By contrast Nisbet interprets the Renaissance as a "flouting of tradition, the spirit of counterculture, and the exaltation of the wayward or dissident."[40] It was the Renaissance, Nisbet suggests, which fostered a new outbreak of belief in "the occult," magic, and fate or fortune. "In their reaction to medieval scholasticism," Nisbet writes, "the humanists were necessarily carried to place an emphasis upon the emotions, passions, and other nonrational affective states which were scarcely compatible with any theory of progress." Then he asks, "How could one be seriously interested in the rational principles—divine or secular in foundation—which underlay ancient and medieval belief in the advancement of man when ideas of luck, chance, and accident flourished in an age of crumbling faith in reason and morality?"[41]

Nisbet's surprising neglect of the major Renaissance theme of this-worldliness, so manifest in its works of art, raises questions once more about the nature of his historical analysis. In short we have in Nisbet's work little more than the advocacy of some sort of moral, religious rebirth, accompanied also by a suggested synthesis of scientific and religious thought. This advocacy is quite clear in his Epilogue. One can, of course, sympathize with Nisbet's concern about aspects of our modern culture, but the question must be asked whether history itself needs to be rewritten, as Nisbet attempts it, for the sake of making a moral statement.[42] One must ask whether the belief in Progress needs to be accorded a dubious antiquity in order to steel thoughtful persons against moral decline.

The scholarly response to Nisbet's book was at best mixed. One reviewer responded enthusiastically and declared that as a result of Nisbet's work, "Bury's book now deserves retirement after long service."[43] But other reviewers were much more critical of Nisbet's work, and one of these described the book as "a scissors-and-paste job, and a dull one, on the history of a great idea."[44] This reviewer went on to observe:

> [Professor Nisbet] tells us "the actual aim" of his book "is that of providing a straightforward history of the idea of progress; from the Greeks to our own day." He knows there is something odd about this proposal, for the learned world is pretty much agreed that the idea of progress is not to be found in European thought much before the seventeenth century. . . . To announce that he is going to maintain, against so many others, that the idea is a commonplace among the Greeks, in St. Augustine, in the Middle Ages, is surely to announce that he intends to give us some hard argument and a close study, and a radical reinterpretation, of the texts and other historical evidences these others found persuasive.[45]

However, the reviewer asserts that none of this is accomplished. Instead "fragments are quoted that bring out the not very contentious claim that the ancients knew that there had been technical and other improvements over historical time and that with the taking of pains they could expect other improvements in time to come."[46] This commonplace view was clearly not regarded by the chief minds of antiquity as a focus of meaning or human hope; and such would have had to be the case if these classical views bore correspondence with the modern belief in Progress. In sum the reviewer, J. M. Cameron, declares forcefully in favor of Bury, and against Nisbet, in reaffirming the *modern* nature of the belief in Progress.

In 1982, following Nisbet's work, another major discussion of the theme of Progress appeared, this time a symposium of views sponsored by the Western Center of the American Academy of Arts and Sciences. There is an unfortunate overlap in this and Nisbet's work since the conference represented by this collection of papers occurred in February 1979, more than a year before the appearance of Nisbet's book. In its final published form, however, some of the papers , along with the introduction, take account of Nisbet's work and offer limited comment. The most instructive of these papers, in terms of the history of the idea of Progress, is that of George G. Iggers, entitled "The Idea of Progress in Historiography and Social Thought Since the Enlightenment."[47] Iggers, who reaffirms the accepted view of Bury that the belief in Progress is essentially a modern, eighteenth-century idea, writes:

> The idea of progress has a specific meaning in the context of the eighteenth, nineteenth, and—to an extent still—the twentieth century which differentiates it essentially from ideas of historical progression in the classical Greek or Roman world or in the Hebraic and Christian traditions. . . . Its appeal was strongest among those sections of the population—particularly of the intelligentsia—that were interested in the transformation of the economy, society and politics from traditional patterns, dominant in the *ancient régime*, to modern conditions of growth.[48]

Iggers then goes on to make the important point that "ideas originate within a concrete social, political and intellectual setting, in part in response to this setting; they are not merely formal concepts but have a specific content that can be understood only with reference to the historical situation." With this statement Iggers registers dissatisfaction with a mere philosophical description of the unfolding of an idea, certainly a distinctive feature of Bury's work. Iggers is concerned to address the problem of why ideas emerge, why they become powerful in the lives of people, why they persist, and then decline. He notes, "If [the idea of Progress] is narrated as a history of ideas, then the question why these ideas changed must be confronted."[49]

Since Iggers' own task, however, is to discuss the idea of Progress in the context of the nineteenth- to twentieth-century European historical situation, he does not go back to supplement Bury's work. He does not offer interpretation of the social, historical "causality" underlying the rise of the belief in Progress. He simply moves on to his own illuminating description of current views of Progress in English, French, and German historiography. In this task, Iggers is concerned to spell out how historians within the separate European traditions have expressed their belief, or lack of belief, in this controlling idea.

In regard to our own purpose of relating the history of the idea of Progress to the question of technology it is important to underline, from the preceding discussion, the consensus view that *the belief in Progress is essentially a modern idea and that though the ancient world of Greece and Rome had some awareness of technological advance this awareness did not spawn the idea of Progress.* Bury's study continues to be helpful in explaining why this was so: the nexus of value commitments[50] and intellectual perceptions in the ancient world were simply not conducive to its conceptual emergence.

Iggers makes an important point in charging that Bury provides little account of the social and historical factors that helped give rise to the idea of Progress. This is a matter that demands at least some elaboration, however abbreviated, for it has important bearing upon the weighting of the technological factor in the formulating of the idea of Progress. Here let us return to the view of Bury and others that Judeo-Christian thought contributed significantly to the rise of the belief in Progress by its projection of a linear concept of history.

This idea that history, all history, was moving toward some kind of final resolution in a divine judgment and fulfillment certainly helped undermine, as Bury proposed, the earlier cyclical view of history; but the point also needed fuller treatment than Bury provided: thus the work of John Baillie,[51] Karl Lowith,[52] and the many who have argued the parallels between secular ideologies and religious millennialist expectations.[53]

Nevertheless overemphasis upon this feature of the religious tradition also raises questions, for certainly the millennialist point of view, though common to certain groups in the fifteenth and sixteenth centuries, was for the most part a secondary feature of medieval religious belief. The much more dominant orientation in the medieval system was belief in life after death, belief that an eternal world hovered over this imperfect material one and that the final goal of human life was to secure the transition of the soul from this world to the next, an event closely tied to the church's sacraments and finally coming to issue in each person's death.[54] This pattern of belief, clearly dominant throughout the Middle Ages and manifest in its art, architecture, and religious practices, helps to account for the dominant role and power of the church during most of the Middle Ages through the fifteenth century.

It is important in this connection to recall that life expectancy during the Middle Ages was about twenty-seven years—and that during the Black Plague of 1348 the population of Europe declined by fully one third. Paul Tillich once observed that three great questions have troubled the Western soul. In late antiquity (the Hellenistic age) he suggests it was the question of death, in the Middle Ages the question of guilt, and in the twentieth century the question of meaninglessness.[55] While Tillich is certainly correct in noting a greater theological emphasis upon guilt in the medieval period than, for example, in the first centuries of the Christian era, it seems also apparent that there was no major de-emphasis of death in the medieval period. Death continued to rule as the central fear and concern. It was only because guilt was allied with death that the former gained its medieval prominence. It was, in fact, the heightened fear of death, fear of punishment in purgatory and hell, which made the sale of indulgences such an effective means of raising revenues. As impressive as the Cathedral of St. Peter in Rome continues to be, a tribute to Renaissance art and piety, it is also, in some measure, a monument to the fear of death in the late Middle Ages, for it was built in large part by the sale of indulgences across Europe. Death and the existence of heaven and hell as immediate realities far outweigh in significance the affirmations of a historical destiny, even when proclaimed in imminent, apocalyptic terms.

Having said this about the Middle Ages of the ninth through the thirteenth centuries, one must also go on to affirm that the Renaissance of the fourteenth and fifteenth centuries gave expression to a new this-worldliness not common to the earlier period. A growing curiosity about the world, the desire to explore and discover "new worlds," an art that presented color and form in new, dynamic ways: these developments reflect a change in mood, a shift in viewpoint to a more positive appraisal of life in this world. Baumer comments on a certain double-mindedness in the Renaissance period: a clinging to the old other-worldly "Aristotelian-Christian universe of purpose and striving" is held in company with a new enjoyment and appreciation of this life. He illustrates this through the person of Petrarch (1307–1374). "Petrarch . . . confesses to being torn apart inside by the claims of two worlds, 'A stubborn and still undecided battle has been long raging on the field of my thoughts for the supremacy of one of the two men within me!—the spiritual man described in St. Augustine's *Confessions*, and the worldly man lusting after literary fame and the beauties of nature.' "[56] And another historian has observed that the revolution in cosmology which occurred in the sixteenth and seventeenth centuries was preceded by a revolution in cartography which occurred during the Renaissance period with the great voyages of discovery.[57] Such are but a few of the marks of a world in transition.

While one can surely argue that the technological-economic advances which occurred during the Middle Ages helped prepare the ground for the shift to a this-worldly consciousness,[58] a problem persists in attempting to account historically for the articulation and then the shared affirmation of this new awareness. Commenting on the exhaustive work of Joseph Needham, *Science and Civilization in China*, Lynn White, Jr., declares: "He [Needham] wants to know why, in different cultures, science and engineering have taken such diverse shapes and have been of such varying significance."[59] White himself attempts an answer to this question in his discussion of possible causes for the speedup of technological change in the West during the Middle Ages, a discussion that accords a significant role to distinctive emphases in the religious orientation of the West.[60]

Our own task is to offer further assessment of the historical factors at work in the formulation of the belief in Progress. Among these is certainly the phenomenon of technological innovation in the West, but also Renaissance curiosity about the world, and, as I will argue, the religious revolution of the sixteenth century. Ignored by Enlightenment thinkers and by later nineteenth-century historians, Jacob Burckhardt especially, but also by Bury, the Reformation helped to set the agenda for the seventeenth- to eighteenth-century world.

Martin Luther, of course, intended no radical social or political upheaval. His own conception of what he was about centered in his preaching of justification by faith, the idea that humankind could be saved not by human effort and striving, but solely by divine grace, God's saving act in the cross of Christ. This accent upon divine grace rather than upon human effort certainly ran counter to the later belief in Progress, in which human will and human goals were seen as the chief hope for human betterment. Luther's emphasis upon grace was also an effort to address the question of motivation in doing the good. He expected that if people understood the nature of God's love they would be stirred, out of gratitude, to good works. Good works would become spontaneous, uncoerced, and a contagious righteousness would permeate all of society. He shunned the thought, however, of change by human design. The status quo was to be changed in the heart, by God's word, and by God's Spirit in the hearing of that word. The preaching of the gospel was understood to be the chief agency for change.

As otherworldly and as spiritual as Luther's doctrine was, it became, however, an occasion of great this-worldly ferment and upheaval, in no small part because of its radical, spiritual egalitarianism. Everyone— pope, cleric, prince, and cobbler—stood equally in need of grace. All stood on the same level in relation to God, all were equally appealed to in sermon, pamphlet, woodcut, and all who responded to God's word, in faith, became believers, "saints." Luther's doctrine was a spiritual assault on the principle of hierarchy, but, of course, he did not intend it to be an assault on the structure of society—not directly. He in fact vehemently forbade such an assault when in 1525 the peasants saw in his preaching a sanction to resist social injustice with force. The vehemence with which Luther turned against the violence of the peasants fixed a pattern for Lutheran quietism in social and political matters that persisted largely unaltered up through World War II.

In two areas, however, Luther's preaching of justification had social-political ramifications which could not be contained within the parameters of a conservative Lutheran social doctrine. The belief in the equality of all persons in relation to the need and promise of grace made irrelevant all special spiritual disciplines which demanded an existence apart from the workaday world. In Lutheran territories the monastic orders became extraneous, and dissolution of such orders soon followed the preaching of justification. Monastery buildings and lands were taken over and used for other purposes, often for education. This redistribution of wealth, its utilization for other, often secular purposes, had wide-ranging political implications. In England, over the course of the English reformation, it became, very clearly, an instrument of political power and leverage.

Over and above this concrete form of social and political change, the redistribution of monastic lands, Luther's reform contributed markedly to the enhancement of political power. Luther relied on the magistracy to help carry through the reform of the church. One historian has described the process in the following terms:

> Princes had always enjoyed a multitude of rights within the church, and long before the Reformation the Duke of Cleves spoke for most German princes when he claimed that in his own lands he was pope and master. Previous reforming princes had made visitations to monasteries, but these were considered as emergency measures and did not affect doctrine. The new visitations . . . undertaken in Saxony and in the territories of other evangelical princes [were] more extensive and [possessed] a theological intent which [made] them channels for the ideas of reform. . . . Luther provided a preface to the visitation articles of 1528. There he explained that only in times of distress may the elector name visitors (political overseers of religious life), and that he does this not by right of his secular

office but as a Christian brother out of love. It was a nice distinction made necessary by the emergency but difficult to maintain.[61]

What is described here is a significantly heightened role for political power in the cultural history of the West. Contrary to Luther's own hopes and expectations, political power—in the form of the princes in Germany—became decisive in determining the "eternal" destiny of the people, at least whether they were to be Catholics, Lutherans, or Reformed. Political power, for many—certainly not all—subtly assumed a new significance and accomplished real changes. The "secularization" of the monasteries was accompanied by a heightened sense of political existence and for politics as an instrument of broad-based change.

The Reformation made clear that there was no longer a dominant institution free from the processes of change. Earlier on, the church had stood as a sort of primal, sacred institution, a symbol of stability and an eternal order. It had long been viewed as standing in need of moral and spiritual reform—with Luther also of doctrinal reform. A further feature of the reform movement, especially in its Calvinist and Anabaptist dimensions, was the recognition that church structure was also subject to major revision. The Calvinists and Anabaptists made clear that alternative, nonhierarchical ecclesiastical structures were not only possible but called for. The lesson became apparent to many that hierarchical political structures, as well as ecclesiastical structures, could no longer claim a divine right. In England the issue was expressed in the adage: "If the bishops go, the monarchy is in trouble," a point the historian Michael Walzer has helped to underline with his analysis of the religious roots of the revolutionary political tradition in the West.[62] Just as the sighting of the new star in 1572 had helped to establish awareness that the heavenly sphere of the fixed stars was subject to change,[63] so the Reformation, earlier, made clear that there was no fixed order for ecclesiastical or political institutions. Unlike the world of ancient Greece and Rome, where change was viewed in negative terms, the Reformation, despite its rather limited successes, helped to further a change in the attitude toward change. Inevitably the awareness grew that the alteration of ecclesiastical, political, and social institutions was, or could become, a human task and a human hope.

As we seek to account for the rise of the belief in Progress, certainly this religious and social history needs telling if the idea of Progress is to be understood as a human commitment and hope—and not only, as Bury tends to represent it, as an unfolding idea. It was an experience of power, an experience of human-initiated historical change, in some measure for the good, which lies behind the rise of the belief in Progress.

And this aspect of the religious revolution of the sixteenth century is essential to the history of the idea.

This is not, however, an end to the social-historical understanding called for in our preceding discussion. There is also, let us suggest, a humanistic rebirth that accompanies the belief in Progress, and here the scientific revolution of the sixteenth and seventeenth centuries plays the crucial role.

Of course, the indispensable role of the scientific revolution in the rise of the belief in Progress has long been stressed. Bury, and every other intellectual historian, has made the point that the shift from a geocentric to a heliocentric view of the world was indeed a revolutionary development—one in fact which led to the subsequent use of the word "revolution" to describe a radical social-political upheaval.[64] To be sure, Bury suggests that with the Renaissance a new intellectual self-confidence began to stir in the West. This is certainly warranted. Criticism of inherited belief began to take place in such figures as Lorenzo Valla (1406–1457) and Pico della Mirandola (1463–1494), but such groping expressions of intellectual self-assertion should not be allowed to diminish the truly epochal intellectual self-discovery that resulted from the Copernican-Newtonian cosmological revolution. Nicolaus Copernicus (1473–1543) began the criticism of the old Ptolemaic, geocentric universe essentially on aesthetic grounds, not on the basis of new data. He complained of a sense of untidiness, incoherencies in the inherited world picture.[65] Johannes Kepler (1571–1630) pressed forward to define the laws of planetary motion on the basis of more precise measurements; and Galileo (1564–1642) helped confirm Copernicus' view with his telescopic observations.

It was Isaac Newton (1642–1727), however, who provided the climactic statement of the new world picture with his definition of the universal law of gravity, his insight that heavenly bodies as well as all earthly objects were bound by one and the same law of nature. Newton's achievement was hailed throughout the world of his day. Upon his death, he was memorialized in the following terms by the poet James Thomson:

> Have ye not listened while he bound the suns
> And planets to their spheres! The unequal task
> Of humankind till then. Oft hand they rolled
> O'er erring man the year, and oft disgraced
> The pride of schools, before their course was known
> Full in its causes and effects to him,
> All-piercing sage![66]

Thomson here expressed the spirit of intellectual liberation which Newton came to represent. The great minds of antiquity, "the pride of schools," might have been excused for not conjuring the geographical extent of their world, but they were certainly to be held to account for the failure to understand the movement of the heavens over their heads. From this point on, the authority and awe of the past were beyond restoration. The present and the future took on new meaning and beckoned to new truths, new achievements.

Science, Newton, the future, took on the cloak of promise not only as possibilities in and of themselves but also by contrast to the tragic legacy of warfare and destruction that followed upon the efforts at religious reform. The sixteenth and seventeenth centuries were ravaged by a series of religious-political wars in France, in the Netherlands, in Germany, in England. If Christianity and its institutional form had proved to be an answer to death and a promise of stability amid all the uncertainties of the earlier Middle Ages, in the sixteenth and seventeenth centuries it became a cause of death and an occasion of political and social instability.

In France from 1562 to 1598, the religious question triggered a pattern of civil strife that exhausted the nation. Historians are still at work trying to assess the scope of the disaster to France. One of the most recent studies concludes:

> It is . . . hard to imagine that the damages sustained by France were or could have been in any sense marginal. The demographic consequences of two partially lost generations of adult males (not to mention females and children) must have been severe, the economic consequences of destruction of resources, long-term disinvestment of capital . . . vast. The developmental consequences of lost opportunities and foregone production, though they can only be calculated imaginatively . . . bespeak a cultural disaster of the largest magnitude.[67]

For almost forty years strategic sections of France suffered forms of "military and civil violence . . . akin to a total disintegration of lawful and ordered society."[68] In the Netherlands, during the war for independence from Catholic Spain (1560–1590s), the Dutch people suffered in like manner. In the end the Protestant northern provinces were able to secure their independence but at great cost. Germany was similarly plundered and torn apart by religious-political strife. The Thirty Years' War (1618–1648) secured Protestantism for the north of Germany, as it did Catholicism in the south, but again at immense cost. A church historian described the conflict in the following terms:

> To Germany the Thirty Years' War was an unmitigated and frightful evil. The land had been ploughed from end to end for a generation by lawless and plundering armies. Population had fallen from sixteen million to less than six. Fields were waste. Commerce and manufacturing destroyed.

Above all intellectual life had stagnated, morals had been roughened and corrupted, and religion grievously maimed. A century after its close the devastating consequences had not been made good.[69]

In short, the evil attending the religious wars that ravaged Europe over the last half of the sixteenth century and throughout most of the seventeenth century was of such magnitude that a profound reaction to religion set in among sensitive, discerning intellectuals. Hope shifted from religion to a "rational politics," and the intellectual self-confidence discovered with the overthrow of the Aristotelian-Ptolemaic worldview became the inspiration for new possibilities of political existence. A liberated rationality could accomplish for politics what it had achieved in the revised understanding of the mechanics of the heavens. Religion, in many intellectual quarters, came to be viewed as a bastion of ignorance and superstition, an evil to be overcome if new possibilities of life were to be secured for this world. Thus Voltaire voiced the hope that he might live to see "the last king throttled in the bowels of the last Jesuit"[70] and Condorcet in declaring for the perfectibility of humankind wrote: "The time will therefore come when the sun will shine only on free men who know no other master but their reason; when tyrants and slaves, priests and their stupid or hypocritical instruments, will exist only in works of history and on the stage; and when we shall think of them only to pity their victims and their dupes."[71] Condorcet asserted that a free people must learn "to recognize and so to destroy, by force of reason, the first seeds of tyranny and superstition, should they ever dare to reappear amongst us."[72] Thus to have Progress an "enemy" needs to be identified and a means of overcoming the enemy defined.

In the seventeenth and eighteenth centuries the course of history had set the agenda for Progress. The field of philosophy responded by defining human meaning and hope in terms of the very large theme of epistemology: How do we know? How is it that we moderns are superior in our knowing to the great minds of the past?—and in terms of political theory: Why should we not define our own destiny? Progress, the new creed, was a statement of hope, which claimed the commitment of the modern age. It was, clearly, a social-political gospel. On this point, George Iggers observes: "Growth for its own sake was never what the idea of progress in its classical form was about. Progress was always conceived in broad social terms. A basic assumption of the theorists of progress has been that 'man is not merely a natural being: he is a *human* natural being.'"[73]

Then how is it that in our time, here in the last decade of the twentieth century, we have come to identify progress chiefly with growth, with technology? It is to this question we turn in the next chapter.

3
DISILLUSION AND POWER

A remarkable little book was published by Yale University Press in the year 1932. The Storr Lectures, presented at the Yale School of Law by a Cornell history professor Carl L. Becker, are an interpretation of the Enlightenment and its belief in Progress. Entitled *The Heavenly City of the Eighteenth-Century Philosophers*, the book has gone through forty-six printings. It is a book that has refused to die. Becker's view of the eighteenth century is especially provocative in that it runs counter to the modern inclination to see the Enlightenment as part and parcel of our contemporary modern outlook.

Becker's startling argument is that the Enlightenment and its belief in Progress is closer in spirit to the Middle Ages than to our own time. Becker states the case:

> And yet I think the *Philosophes* [the intellectual spokesmen of the Enlightenment] were nearer the Middle Ages, less emancipated from the preconceptions of medieval Christian thought, than they quite realized or we have commonly supposed. If we have done them more (or is it less?) than justice in giving them a good modern character, the reason is that they speak a familiar language. We read Voltaire more readily than Dante, and follow an argument by Hume more easily than one by Thomas Aquinas. But I think our appreciation is of the surface more than of the fundamentals of their thought. We agree with them more readily when they are witty and cynical than when they are wholly serious. Their negations rather than their affirmations enable us to treat them as kindred spirits.[1]

Becker maintains that such Enlightenment figures as Montesquieu, Voltaire, Rousseau, Diderot, d'Holbach, Condorcet, may have scorned the religious past, but they subtly preserved many of the essentials of that past. As Becker states it:

> They . . . put off the fear of God, but [preserved] a respectful attitude toward the Deity. They ridiculed . . . [a six-day creation], but still be-

lieved [the universe] to be a beautifully articulated machine designed by the Supreme Being. . . . The Garden of Eden was for them a myth, no doubt, but they looked enviously back to the golden age of Roman virtue, or across the waters to the unspoiled innocence of an Arcadian civilization . . . in Pennsylvania. They renounced the authority of church and Bible, but exhibited a naïve faith in the authority of nature and reason. . . . They denied that miracles ever happened, but believed in the perfectibility of the human race.[2]

Posterity, or the future, became for the eighteenth-century "enlightened" what the other world was for the religious. The "City of God" became a project. Everything became a project. Becker comments on how the Abbé de Saint-Pierre, an Enlightenment figure, provided a fount of "projects."

How many "projects" he wrote, helpful hints for the improvement of mankind—"Project for Making Roads Passable in Winter," "Project for the Reform of Begging," "Project for Making Dukes and Peers Useful." And then one day, quite suddenly, so he tells us, "there came into my mind a project which by its great beauty struck me with astonishment. It has occupied all my attention for fifteen days." The result . . . : *A Project for Making Peace Perpetual in Europe*.[3]

Becker argues that this passion for projects from the *Encyclopedia* to the French Revolution was the distinctive mark of the Enlightenment: "With earnest purpose, with endless argument and impassioned propaganda and a few not unhappy tears shed in anticipation of posterity's gratitude, [the eighteenth century] devoted all its energies to sketching the most naïvely simple project ever seen for making dukes and peers useful, for opening all roads available to the pursuit of happiness, for securing the blessings of liberty, equality, and fraternity to all mankind." Pressing his analysis of the close kinship of the Enlightenment with the religious perspective of the Middle Ages, Becker concludes that what lay behind this eighteenth-century commitment to projects and "Progress" was "the Christian ideal of service, the humanitarian impulse to set things right."[4]

In the subsequent course of his lectures Becker buttressed this analysis with historical documentation on how Enlightenment thinkers sketched out a picture of the world they longed for—a world not of God—but of "Nature." And a very select "history," determined by the philosophes, became a source of "revelation," providing the blueprint for what the world was to become under the rubric of Progress.

Becker's representation of these aspects of eighteenth-century thought elicited a variety of responses from his scholarly peers. Almost all the early reviews remarked on Becker's erudition and wit. A philosopher-critic took issue with some fine points in Becker's reading of the history of philosophy—and really missed the point of the book.[5] The *Times Literary Supplement* review accented Becker's intelligence and charm but suggested that in the Middle Ages faith was joined with reason and in the Enlightenment reason was joined with faith.[6] In the *American Historical Review*, Becker's professional colleague, the historian Charles Beard, offered a brief, bland review that gave little substantive comment and closed with the usual word of praise for Becker's "beautifully finished literary project."[7]

The reviewer for the *Times Literary Supplement* suggested that along with all the wit and charm of Becker's work some readers were likely to find the approach a little "irritating." The reviewer, unfortunately, did not spell out what he meant by this comment. Subsequent interest in Becker's interpretation became the occasion for a scholarly review and reassessment of the book in 1956, about eleven years after Becker's death.[8] Held in connection with a professional meeting of historians, the symposium provided opportunity for a group of younger historians, along with some from Becker's own generation, to enter into dialogue about the validity of Becker's interpretation of the Enlightenment. At the conference considerable negative criticism was voiced especially in the person of Peter Gay, a well-known Enlightenment authority. Gay's remarks were aimed chiefly to rebut Becker's charge that the Enlightenment philosophers were "religious"—but here, he too missed Becker's point.[9] Becker certainly does not argue that the philosophes, with their belief in Progress, were "Christian" in any fundamental sense of that term, only that they might be described as "true believers" in their enthusiastic commitment to the secular alternative to Christian belief. This is made abundantly clear by Becker when, in his lectures, he enumerates the major tenets of Enlightenment "religion" that "(1) man is not natively depraved; (2) the . . . [purpose] of life is life itself, the good life on earth instead of the beatific life after death; (3) man is capable, guided solely by the light of reason and experience, of perfecting the good life on earth; and (4) the first and essential condition of the good life on earth is the freeing of men's minds from the bonds of ignorance and superstition, and of their bodies from the arbitrary oppression of the constituted social authorities."[10]

Peter Gay was not alone in his misreading of Becker and what he was about. But what *is* clear from the twenty-five-year review of Becker's "Heavenly City" is that Becker's capacity to stimulate, "irritate," people continued unabated. And what seems most irritating about his perspective is that Becker himself was manifestly an "unbeliever," an unbeliever not only in the Christian faith of the Middle Ages (and later) but also in the dubiously "rational" belief in Progress which had so inspired the Enlightenment philosophers. This is a point that demands further discussion.

In his brief 1933 review of Becker's book, Charles Beard *did* offer one important observation, that Becker in his lectures deals with a comparison not of two periods of history but of three: the Middle Ages, the Enlightenment, *and* the twentieth century. This is a matter which many of Becker's critics in the 1956 symposium clearly missed. Becker writes from the perspective of a twentieth-century nihilism which many of his contemporaries simply did not share. The term "nihilism" may be too strong here, since Becker obviously believed in *some* things, but not those tenets of Enlightenment belief which stirred the enthusiasm of the eighteenth century and continued to claim important loyalties into the twentieth century. Becker had clearly abandoned the social and political optimism of the Enlightenment belief in Progress and thus spoke about this belief as an outsider. It is this issue which irritates some, perhaps many, of Becker's readers and comes to the fore in Gay's closing 1956 assessment of Becker. Gay complains: "In his impatience with his intellectual forebears . . . he portrayed the *philosophes* as naïve and as a little fraudulent. Becker was no conservative, but the conservative implications of *The Heavenly City* are plain."[11] Whether or not Becker charges the Enlightenment philosophes with being "fraudulent" is open to question, but Gay's final complaint is patently a political one. Gay is concerned that Becker's quasi-nihilistic reading of history tends to undermine the liberal-progressive political commitment and that such a perspective might encourage a neoconservative, even a fascist point of view. Yet this was precisely the gist of Becker's analysis of Enlightenment history writing: it was made to serve their vision of the world. Gay simply did not share—or want to share—Becker's reading of the twentieth-century historical situation because it was politically unacceptable.

Despite some paucity, some brevity in the argument, there are two reasons for Becker's twentieth-century cynicism, which distance him from the Enlightenment outlook. One is a troubled acceptance of the late nineteenth-, early twentieth-century view of the universe. This view, based upon the law of entropy, maintained that energy is constantly moving from a more to a less ordered and useful state, with the result that the universe is winding down and is due to suffer its own "death." (Energy is conserved but it is too diffuse to sustain life.) Becker quotes Bertrand Russell on this point.

> That man is the product of causes which had no prevision of the end they were achieving; that his origin, his growth, his hopes and fears, his loves and his beliefs, are but the outcome of accidental collocations of atoms;

that all the labours of all the ages, all the devotion, all the inspiration, all
the noonday brightness of human genius are destined to extinction in the
vast death of the solar system . . . —all these things, if not quite beyond
dispute, are yet so nearly certain that no philosophy which rejects them
can hope to stand.[12]

Becker himself comments: "What is man that the electron should be
mindful of him! Man is but a foundling in the cosmos, abandoned
by the forces that created him. Unparented, unassisted and undirected
by omniscient or benevolent authority, he must fend for himself, and
with the aid of his own limited intelligence find his way about in an
indifferent universe." "Such," Becker declares, "is the world pattern
that determines the character and direction of modern thinking."[13] Such
a view is also far distant from the Enlightenment embrace of nature as
the abiding home for the human spirit.

It is not only this scientific account of the system of nature but also
the cumulative experience of history—this especially—which stands as
bar to Becker's endorsement of the Enlightenment belief in Progress.
His sober summation of the course of events since the eighteenth century makes clear the source of his cynicism. Becker writes:

After the [French] Revolution had spent its fury, faith in the new religion
of humanity lost much of its mystic and perfervid quality. Still it lived on,
inspiring, in the new world and in the old, many lesser revolutions; and it
had even one great revival before and during the splendid debacle of
1848.[14]

Becker goes on:

The German Empire, the third French Republic, the Kingdom of Italy,
the Austro-Hungarian "Compromise," a "household suffrage" thrown as
a sop to tenants on entailed estates—these, and similar tarnished imita-
tions, were the "rewards" which posterity, after a century of enlightenment, grudgingly bestowed upon the impassioned propagandists and
martyrs of the democratic faith. The great Revolution, as an accomplished fact, betrayed the hopes of its prophets, the Rousseaus and the
Condorcets, the Robespierres and the Rolands, the Mazzinis and
the Kossuths. No doubt the illusion of its prophets was to suppose
that the evil propensities of men would disappear with the traditional
forms through which they functioned. Before the end of the nineteenth
century, at all events, it was obvious that the abolition of old oppres-
sions and inequities had done little more than make room for new
ones.[15]

We have quoted Becker at length because one sees here how deeply he
was himself gripped by historical disillusion. And it was out of this
disenchantment with Enlightenment dreams that Becker's cynicism

grew—that cynicism which so irritated those, like Gay, who still longed to believe with some measure of Enlightenment enthusiasm.

In a later work, written in 1936, Becker identifies with greater precision the occasion of his disillusion.

> For two centuries the Western world has been sustained by a profound belief in the doctrine of progress. Although God the Father had withdrawn into the places where Absolute Being dwells, it was still possible to maintain that the Idea or Dialectic or Natural Law, functioning through the conscious purposes or the unconscious activities of men, could be counted on to safeguard mankind against future hazards. However formulated, with whatever apparatus of philosophic or scientific terminology defended, the doctrine was in essence an emotional conviction, a species of religion—a religion which according to Professor Bury, served as a substitute for the declining faith in the Christian doctrine of salvation: "The hope of an ultimate happy state on this planet to be enjoyed by future generations . . . has replaced, as a social power, the hope of felicity in another world."
>
> Since 1918 this hope has perceptibly faded. Standing within the deep shadow of the Great War, it is difficult to recover the nineteenth-century faith either in the fact or the doctrine of progress.[16]

The designation of World War I as a watershed event in the history of the idea of Progress, progress at least as a doctrine of political and social hope, will be contested by many. Because World War I led also to the Bolshevik accession to power in Russia, many committed Marxists, those of Marxist-Leninist persuasion, would not and could not identify World War I as a negative turning point, one of decline. Quite the contrary it became a moment of great hope for most committed Marxists, but for increasing numbers throughout the non-Marxist, Western world, anxiety and meaninglessness replaced political hope as a persistent dimension of the social-political realm. Intellectual historians have often described the post–World War I period of Western history as "the age of anxiety,"[17] and certainly existentialism as a broadly based cultural outlook finds its origins here. With World War I, Christian thought, responding to the same historical realities, also underwent a radical transformation in the turn to neo-orthodoxy. We speak here of the theological work of such figures as Karl Barth, Rudolf Bultmann, Emil Brunner, Paul Tillich, and in America, Reinhold Niebuhr.

A highly praised study of the impact of the war upon English literature further establishes the tragic nature of World War I as a cultural event of major proportion. Paul Fussell, in *The Great War and Modern Memory*, points out how tastes in literature were altered over the course of the conflict. He notes that as a result of the military stalemate on the Western front and because of the nature of trench warfare, there were lengthy periods of relative quiet between major offensives. In an effort to maintain the morale of the troops during these periods of quiet, the separate governments, especially the English, deluged the troops with books and other reading materials. On the literary nature of the war, Fussell observes:

> In 1914 there was virtually no cinema; there was no radio at all. . . . Except for sex and drinking, amusement was largely found in language formally arranged, either in books or periodicals or at the theater and music hall, or in one's own or one's friends' anecdotes, rumors, or clever structuring of words. It is hard for us to recover imaginatively such a world, but we must imagine it if we are to understand the way "literature" dominated the war from beginning to end.[18]

He then goes on to describe the response of the troops to the English government's effort at providing reading material—and how literary tastes changed.

> In producing a multi-volume "Service" Kipling, the publishers badly misestimated the literary inclinations of those on the line. *Kim* was fairly popular, but most of the troops preferred anything of Conrad's, perhaps because, as Pilditch felt, his works offered characters caught in something like the troops' own predicament, people "who played their parts, half ignorant and yet half realizing the inexorable march of fate and their own insignificance before it." It was the same instinct for dark and formal irony that turned the soldiers to Hardy. Sassoon speaks for the whole British Expeditionary Force when he says, "I didn't want to die—not before I'd finished *The Return of the Native* anyhow."[19]

With the change in taste, there occurred also a change in vocabulary, though this came about more gradually. Here reference is made to the death of nineteenth-century romantic vocabulary in which a friend was a "comrade," a horse a "steed," the enemy the "foe," to conquer was to "vanquish," to be cheerfully brave was to be "plucky." The list of words that "died" in the war is a long one.[20] The harsh reality of the war swept this diction aside and in its stead came the common words of those who lived and died in the war. Ernest Hemingway summed it up, eleven years after the war, in *A Farewell to Arms*: "Abstract words such as glory, honor, courage, or hallow were obscene beside the concrete names of villages, the numbers of roads, the names of rivers, the numbers of regiments and the dates."[21]

Lest one fall victim to the "abstract," the theoretical, in this effort to understand the impact of World War I, a straightforward description of the struggle from a standard history text presents an overview of the horror.

The youth of England, France, and Germany was squandered upon each other's fixed positions. In this fantastic new form of warfare, men lived like foxes and moles, in burrows that were sometimes only a score of yards from those of their adversaries. . . . Periodically, the high command, with an enthusiasm and optimism that never seemed to die, ordered a general offensive in this or that sector of the front. These big pushes were preceded by a protracted artillery barrage that was intended to flatten the enemy's wire, destroy as many of his strong points as possible, and leave his troops cowering in their trenches in a state of shock. . . . When these preparatory steps were complete, the infantry began to go over the top of their parapets in waves and, with fixed bayonets, and under a rolling barrage, to walk toward the enemy trenches. All too often it was discovered at this point that the barrage had not been long enough to do what it was expected to do, or that the enemy had withdrawn from the shelled lines and was now fighting back from intact ones, or that the bombardment had turned the battlefield into a swamp that made movement impossible. . . . As a result, the gains were always infinitesimal and the losses tremendous.[22]

The writer continues:

During all of 1915, for instance, despite repeated attacks the British and French did not gain more than three miles at any one point; but the French suffered 1,430,000 casualties. Falkenhayn hammered at Verdun for ten months in 1916 and did not take it, but lost 336,000 men. In the battle of the Somme in the same year, the Allies lost 614,000 men and the Germans 650,000 without any appreciable gain on either side. In the third battle of Ypres in 1917, the British fought for five months and, with casualties of 450,000, advanced less than five miles on a nine-mile front.[23]

The total estimated number of dead in the war is staggering, almost all of them young men: 2,000,000 Germans, 1,350,000 French, 1,340,000 Austro-Hungarians, 1,000,000 British, 640,000 Italians, perhaps 2,250,000 Russians.

Profound disillusion and cynicism grew out of the war. In the midst of the conflict, Henry James, the British writer, spoke for many when he wrote to a friend:

The plunge of civilization into this abyss of blood and darkness . . . is a thing that so gives away the whole long age during which we have supposed the world to be, with whatever abatement, gradually bettering, that to have to take it all now for what the treacherous years were all the while really making for and *meaning* is too tragic for any words.[24]

And another writer, Philip Gibbs, drawing on his own experience of the war, offered the following description of black humor among the troops.

The more revolting it was, the more [people] shouted with laughter. It was . . . the laughter of mortals at the trick which had been played on them by an ironical fate. They had been taught to believe that the whole object of life was to reach out to beauty and love, and that mankind, in its progress to perfection, had killed the beast instinct, cruelty, blood-lust, the primitive, savage law of survival by tooth and claw and club and ax. All poetry, all art, all religion had preached this gospel and this promise.

Now that ideal was broken like a china vase dashed to the ground. The contrast between That and This was devastating. . . . The war-time humor of the soul roared with mirth at the sight of all that dignity and elegance despoiled.[25]

For many the belief in Progress could never be regained—at least in its social and political aspects, the roots from which it first grew. Meaning had thereafter to be redefined in terms other than a perfected humanity gradually being realized in league with the liberal-democratic, political process. True, as already suggested, more than a few academics and literary figures and many laboring people were able to refashion political hope out of the rise to power of Marxism in Russia. The thought that radical reorganization of economic life might be the key to a more fulfilling human future gripped and inspired many, but for most others, such a dream also smacked of illusion and yielded to cynicism.

Carl Becker belonged to this latter group. In the closing pages of his 1932 book he remarks on the uncertain future, wondering whether the hopes that had led up to the French Revolution and then had been severely blighted by the Great War might possibly be restored by the Russian Revolution. Speaking of Soviet Communism, Becker says:

Will the new religion (call it a religion of humanity or of inhumanity as you like) make its way, however, gradually, against whatever opposition, by whatever concessions and compromises, with whatever abatement of fanaticism and ruthlessness, and become in its turn the accepted and the conventional faith? It is possible. . . . It is possible that within a hundred years a regulated economy (call it communism or collective planning as you like) may be recognized throughout the western world as the indispensable foundation of social order, peace and prosperity, the welfare of mankind.[26]

While Becker allowed the possibility that " 'posterity,' in the year 2032, . . . [might celebrate] the events of November, 1917, as a happy turning point in the history of human freedom,"[27] there is no question that this was not Becker's expectation. He concluded his lectures with the question:

Are we to suppose that the Russian Revolution of the twentieth century, like the French Revolution of the eighteenth, is but another stage in the progress of mankind toward perfection? Or should we think, with Marcus Aurelius, that "the man of forty years, if he has a grain of sense, in view of this sameness has seen all that has been and shall be"?[28]

It was with Marcus Aurelius that Becker felt compelled to side.

Here, one must note a difference in the cynicism which Becker had earlier cited as a spiritual link between persons living in the twentieth century and the philosophes of the eighteenth century. In his opening lecture Becker remarked: "We agree with them more readily when they are witty and cynical than when they are wholly serious."[29] While cynicism may be ascribed in fair measure to Voltaire, it is not properly applied to the philosophes as a group, for Becker makes their enthusiastic belief in the future the chief feature setting them off from the post–World War I point of view. When the Enlightenment philosophers attacked religion and the *ancien régime* they did so more in terms of ridicule than cynicism. They believed that religion ("superstition") and ignorance were the main obstacles to be overcome if the human race were to achieve its potential for improvement. Thus, their cynicism was modest, their scorn and ridicule of religion strong.

Another point needs to be made here, a simple point often overlooked and one that Becker better illustrates than he himself made clear. It is this which joins the Enlightenment closer to the modern outlook than Becker allowed. It is the matter of the shift from the other world to this world as the focus of meaning. Becker rather treats this shift of focus from eternity to the future as one of simple substitution. The goals are simply altered, relocated as it were. The "heavenly city" becomes the future society to which the "enlightened" hoped to guide the rest of humanity. But not enough attention has been paid to the social psychology that accompanied this shift. In point of fact a new factor of major historical import was brought into play, the factor of disillusionment.

Disillusionment is a modern malady, one essentially unknown in the religious age, in the medieval period. *The Oxford English Dictionary*, 1933 edition, helps to underline this point by noting that the word "disillusion" begins to come into wide use only with the nineteenth century. The explanation for this is quite simply that if eternity is viewed as the final human goal and the focus of meaning, there is and can be no disillusion. No one comes back to tell a struggling humanity that the goal is not worth the good works and sacrifice expended to attain it. Karl Marx, of course, criticized the belief in eternity as a delusion, but it never led to disillusion. When, however, human dreams and hopes are translated into strictly this-worldly "projects," disillusion becomes a historical factor of major note. Historical experience becomes a judgment upon past hopes and raises the question whether there is *any* hope, in the light of past and present disappointments, which can be steadfastly maintained and for which people can be expected to continue to sacrifice.

If one goes back to Bury's analysis of why the belief in Progress did not arise in the ancient world, one of the arguments put forth was that the ancients lacked sufficient historical perspective to formulate the idea of Progress. The same argument should be kept in mind when assessing the optimism and enthusiasm of the philosophes. They had come to believe that ignorance and superstition, imbedded in the social and political institutions of the old order, the church and the monarchy, were the root causes of humanity's past failure to progress. By ridding humanity of priests and idle kings they believed that the human race would be freed for great new cultural, political advance. In retrospect this belief seems naive but in terms of the eighteenth century, before the French Revolution, there were many who believed it a very reasonable hope, especially against the background of the intolerance and inhumanity of the sixteenth and seventeenth centuries. Becker himself states well this "reasonable" expectation. After noting Edward Gibbon's analysis of the decline and fall of the Roman Empire, which fixed upon "barbarism and religion" as the twin causes for the death of ancient civilization, Becker observed:

> Barbarism and religion. The words fittingly call up the past as imagined by the philosophical century. It was as if mankind, betrayed by barbarism and religion, had been expelled from nature's Garden of Eden. The Christian Middle Ages were the unhappy times after the fall and expulsion, the unfruitful, probationary centuries when mankind, corrupted and degraded by error, wandered blindly under the yoke of oppression. But mankind has at last emerged, or is emerging, from the dark wilderness of the past into the bright, ordered world of the eighteenth century. From this high point of the eighteenth century the Philosophers survey the past and anticipate the future.[30]

And why not? No prior age had defined meaning in terms of this world as did the eighteenth century. No age before the eighteenth century had affirmed, quite like the Enlightenment, that "the . . . [purpose] of life is life itself, the good life on earth instead of the beatific life after death."[31] The philosophes laid the ground for disillusion; thus one ought not accuse them of being "overcredulous." Becker says, "We feel that they are too easily persuaded, that they are naïve souls after all, duped by their humane sympathies, on every occasion hastening to the gate to meet and welcome platitudes and thin panaceas." Becker then declares, "And so our jaded and somewhat morbid modern curiosity is at last aroused. We wish to know the reason for all this fragile optimism."[32] But here Becker's argument gives expression to the ahistorical. It was only the historical experience of the nineteenth and the terrible second decade of the twentieth century that made the Enlightenment philosophes seem "overcredulous." Disillusion as a major actor in the play of history had yet to step on stage and expose the optimism as "fragile." The philosophes would have needed fifty, or seventy, perhaps one hundred and fifty years of historical experience to make the judgment Becker required.

It was not Marcus Aurelius who instructed Becker in a timeless truth; it was the history of the first decades of the twentieth-century world that made clear to him the truth in Aurelius' words: "The man of forty years, if he has a grain of sense, in view of this sameness has seen all that has been and shall be."[33] Or as Henry James put it in 1916: "The plunge of civilization into this abyss of blood and darkness . . . is a thing that so gives away the whole long age during which we have supposed the world to be . . . gradually bettering."[34] Or Philip Gibbs: "Now that ideal was broken like a china vase dashed to the ground. The contrast between That and This was devastating. . . . The war-time humor of the soul roared with mirth at the sight of all that dignity and elegance despoiled."[35]

Becker, however, was ill at ease in nihilism. He wrestled with the question of what was left after the political hope had been shattered. Even Peter Gay, so irritated by Becker's charge of Enlightenment credulity, pointed out that Becker, himself, was "no conservative." What was left? The answer, for Becker—and for many others—was technology.

In 1935, four years after the Yale lectures, Becker gave another, less noted lecture series entitled "Progress and Power." In three lecture sessions, he sought to lay out the groundwork for a very modest message of hope. Becker argued that technology, set against the backdrop of an overview of the human story, provides the most assured basis for a doctrine of Progress. Bound to what he continually refers to as "matter-of-fact knowledge," Becker argued that the mastery of power is the one incontestable development integral to the history of Homo sapiens.[36] Dividing that history into four periods on the basis of major technological advances, Becker suggests that the first 450,000 years of his 506,000-year time scale was distinguished by the use of hand tools. The second period of 50,000 years was featured by the mastery of fire, seeds, the building of shelters and the domestication of animals; the third period of 5,000 years by the development of writing; and the fourth and final period, of less than 1,000 years, by the command of new sources of power, beginning with magnetism but advancing at an accelerated rate with the development of artificial explosives, the steam engine, gas, electricity, and "radiation."[37]

Becker adds dimension to his argument when he asserts that there is a correlation between each major technological advance and an "expansion" of human intelligence. He rejects the attempt to determine a priority for either the technological innovation or the advance in intelligence. He argues:

> The first Ape-Man to learn that an edged flint could be used for cutting may have learned this momentous truth because he was more intelligent than his fellow-apes or he may have become more intelligent than his fellow-apes because his more flexible hand enabled him to verify this momentous truth. We note the correlation and we note that it holds throughout the Time-Scale: the expansion of human intelligence appears to be as much conditioned by the multiplication of implements of power as the multiplication of implements of power is conditioned by the expansion of human intelligence.[38]

Thus Becker offers in his treatment of each major period a description of the technological advances and also a description of the expanded human intelligence occurring within that period. There is imagination and speculation at work in Becker's effort to describe the "expansion of human intelligence," but his effort is nonetheless thought-provoking. What is critical in the whole of Becker's analysis, however, is his treatment of the most recent one thousand years of human history and what he interprets to have been going on in this period down to the present. This is the time period in which the development of the idea of Progress takes place—and Becker represents it in much the same terms as Bury.[39] But Becker's view of what has been going on in the nineteenth and early twentieth centuries is more anxious and troubled than Bury's—more disillusioned, but not wholly.

Again, as he did in *The Heavenly City*, Becker describes a naturalistic metaphysic, one essentially alien to the human spirit. Claiming a cosmic perspective, Becker writes about the earthly setting of the human enterprise.

> We look out upon a universe that comprises perhaps a billion galaxies, each galaxy comprising perhaps ten thousand million stars. If we look long and attentively we may detect, within one of the lesser galaxies, one of the lesser stars which is called the sun; and, circling round this sun, one of its lesser planets which is called the earth. At some moment, relatively early, in the 150,000 million years which is the sun's span of life, we note that certain bits of matter on the surface of the earth, by virtue of temperatures not elsewhere obtaining, assume unusually complicated forms and behave in unusually unstable ways. We understand that certain of these bits of animated dust distinguish themselves from others, dignify themselves with the name of Man, and take credit for having a unique quality which they call intelligence. They are not aware that intelligence is no merit; the reverse rather, since it is only an inferior form of energy which Nature has given them in partial compensation for the extreme rapidity with which

the law of entropy . . . degrades their vitality. . . . Their activities, however long continued, are infinitesimal in extent and impotent in effect, of
no consequence to the universe.[40]

It perhaps goes without saying that Becker's positivistic, naturalistic
metaphysic is dated and that some contemporary "scientific" views,
drawing in part upon the work of Alfred North Whitehead, have presented a universe much more hospitable to human intelligence.[41] But
Becker's primary orientation, as argued earlier, was history and what
chiefly troubled Becker in 1935 was the reality of historical disillusion.
In his continuing narrative of the "progress" of man, Becker describes
the course of events in the nineteenth and into the twentieth century.

The new power discovered by scientists and mediated by engineers is
applied to all the diverse activities of men, but its most notable manifesta-
tions are in the realm of the mechanic and industrial arts. Within this
realm the function of the new power is to accelerate the movement of men
and things and thereby increase work done in relation to the time and the
man-power required to do it.[42]

Continuing this narrative, Becker observes:

We note an unprecedented acceleration in man's capacity to create material wealth; we note also that as instruments of power and precision multiply and are improved, the manpower required to create wealth declines.
Men are themselves aware of these significant facts, and they look forward
to the moment when, with slight effort on their part instruments of power
and precision will supply all that is needed: the moment when common
men, hitherto condemned to live by unremitting labor, will have leisure
for the pursuit of immaterial values, and can live . . . free from toil. . . .
    Nevertheless, from generation to generation the happy moment recedes
and the hopes of men are disappointed.[43]

Becker complains that there is an increasing discrepancy between "the
revolution in scientific knowledge" and "the social revolution that runs
parallel to it." The early optimism is "not justified in the events. It turns
out that men are less tolerant of projects interesting to social reformers
than things are of theories interesting to natural scientists." Becker concludes, "[Thus] . . . while man's effort to control the forces of Nature is
accompanied by increasing success and mounting optimism, his efforts
to regenerate society lead only to confusion and despair."[44]
    Writing in the midst of the Great Depression, Becker accents the
economic problem, especially the inequitable distribution of wealth, but
he sees beyond this to a problem posed by technology. The problem is
that the human race has entered "a new phase of human progress—a
time in which the acquisition of new implements of power too swiftly

outruns the necessary adjustments of habits and ideas to the novel conditions created by their use."[45]

There emerges at this point in Becker's argument a forthright statement of an elitist perspective, something implicit in his earlier treatment of the Enlightenment but now rather baldly put. He suggests that the major problem posed for modern society is that "scientific matter-of-fact knowledge" commanded by the "exceptional few" cannot be applied to human relations and society "without the compliance of the untutored masses." The masses are still too much bound to the past means of establishing social cohesion, to wit: "a common faith in doctrines authoritatively taught."[46] In the past, Becker argues, the sophisticated, learned segment of society, "the priests and scribes," functioned "to stabilize custom and validate social authority by perpetuating the tradition and interpreting it in a manner conformable to the understanding of common men." But more recently, in the past three hundred years, the sophisticated and learned segment of society, now the scientists and technicians, are concerned "to increase rather than to preserve knowledge, to undermine rather than to stabilize custom and social authority."[47] This sophisticated segment of society, in Becker's view, is able to assimilate the new matter-of-fact knowledge and adjust with equanimity to the reality described by that knowledge. They are able to "dispense with traditional views of the origins, the character, and the destiny of man" and to live in "a universe that is as unaware of [man] as of itself and as indifferent to his fate as to its own."[48] But, "common men are not at home" in such an enlarged and basically silent world.

> No longer sustained by traditional doctrines authoritatively taught, and yet incapable by themselves of applying the scientific apprehension to the problems presented by a society so complex and so unstable, they wander aimless and distrait in a shadowy realm of understanding, alternately enticed by venerable faiths that are suspect but not wholly renounced and by the novel implications of factual knowledge accepted on rumor but not understood. . . . Truth emerges from an agreement of minds, and for common men minds agree most effectively when bodies act in unison. Myriad hands lifted in salute are more convincing than facts or syllogisms.[49]

While allowing that some of the despair and social dislocation was the result of inequities in the distribution of wealth, Becker argues that "underlying and conditioning the conflict of material interest between the few and the many is the profound discord between the sophisticated and the unsophisticated levels of apprehension."[50]

As for the future, Becker saw hope in three areas. First, he suggested that taking the long view, the view of "506,000 years of human history," it was evident that matter-of-fact knowledge continually advances and this occurs even against the backdrop of the rise and fall of civilizations. Second, more immediately, he speculated that economic distress and the increasing discipline of the machine would gradually force the common man to abandon "fiction and fancy" and address the realities of existence with a growing pragmatism. Third, he expressed hope that the rate of technological innovation would perhaps level off, ease the pressures of social dislocation, and allow for gradual social adjustment to the more recent, great patterns of change.[51]

What is to be said of this 1935 effort by Becker to deal with the problem of disillusion and refashion a modest hope? Certainly, with regard to the first hope, Becker's broad confidence in positivism and matter-of-fact knowledge, one must observe that this confidence has waned considerably since 1935. Not that practical pragmatic know-how has by any means declined; it still serves as the chief agent in technological growth. But Becker's assumption of scientific commitment to this kind of knowledge and reasoning has not stood the test of time. The modes of scientific reasoning are much more diverse than Becker supposed. Thomas Kuhn, for example, opened up widespread discussion of this matter in his book *The Structure of Scientific Revolutions*.[52] Here Kuhn argued that social and historical factors often play a crucial role in shifting "scientific paradigms." The sources of inspiration in science, as well as other disciplines, are varied and often unpredictable. More recently, it has been suggested that cosmological theory may entirely escape empirical verification, thus necessitating reliance upon "elegance" as the final measure of truth.[53]

In addition Becker's assumption of a "disinterested" elite, wholly adjusted to matter-of-fact knowledge, is seriously to be questioned, if indeed it is to be entertained at all. Becker never lived to learn of the atomic bomb. He spoke of radiation as a newly discovered source of power but he understood this phenomenon in terms of Roentgen's discovery of X-rays, not in terms of nuclear power. The history of the Manhattan Project during World War II indicates that the scientific community, just like every other human community, can become obsessed with its role and fall prey to the temptations of power. In fact, the scientific community possesses no special competence in political judgment.[54] Events since the dropping of the first atomic bomb have done little to restore the tarnished social image of the scientific community—especially in the light of such further problems as toxic waste and the scramble for commercial gain in the field of genetic engineering. Becker's embrace of a "value-free" matter-of-fact knowledge, in the perspective of an additional fifty years, has taken on its own wishful, naive quality.

In like vein, serious questions have to be raised about Becker's second hope: the idea that the machines which we have created on the basis of matter-of-fact knowledge will in time teach us to think in a matter-of-fact way. We have just raised a question as to whether "matter-of-fact thinking" is an adequate description of the dynamics of human thought, whether value-free thought is even a desired, if possible, enterprise. In the following chapter discussion will center specifically on the question of technology and values, but here let us pursue briefly some lines of thought which bear upon Becker's suggestion that machines might eventually correct a deficient human rationality and teach people how properly to "think" and "adjust."

Since 1935 at least two lines of thought emerge which can be viewed as expressing Becker's "technological hope." The first is the proposal that we should develop techniques for controlling the unsophisticated masses by means of behavior modification, psychological techniques for "adjusting" human beings to approved social behaviors. Though Becker spoke of machines doing the schooling of the mind, to the degree that he saw the problem chiefly centered in the unsophisticated masses it is reasonable to assume that he would have approved control of "the masses" through psychological techniques—of course, a control for the good, as in B. F. Skinner's *Walden Two* and *Beyond Freedom and Dignity*.[55] This is a fair surmise though again one should be mindful of Becker's rejection of the fascist option, an option which he regarded, naively it would appear, as a peculiar propensity of the unsophisticated: "for common men minds agree most effectively when bodies act in unison. Myriad hands lifted in salute are more convincing than facts."[56]

The second development since 1935 which perhaps corresponds more closely to Becker's technological hope is the idea that machines, especially communication technology, can shape the way we think. In his 1964 book *Understanding Media*,[57] Marshall McLuhan argued a form of this hope when he proposed that the mode in which we receive information is in the end more significant than the information received. In describing the development of communication technology, from alphabet to printing press to television, McLuhan maintained that human thought has been refashioned by the medium through which information has been received. This argument of McLuhan, which became such a fashion in the mid-1960s, can be viewed in some ways as an elaboration and qualification of the last two stages of human development in Becker's grand 506,000-year overview—the 5,000-year period dominated by writing and the last 1,000 years dominated by the discovery of new sources of power. Becker, of course, wrote only at the beginnings of the "radio age" and he did not anticipate the advent of television, the focus of McLuhan's analysis; but his realistic disposition might have served as a check on McLuhan's romantic exaggeration of the communication media. He would have likely held soberly to the stark actualities of nuclear power, genetic engineering, and the most recent developments in superconductivity. He also would have resisted, I think, abandonment of his initial point in the Progress lectures, the refusal to assert causal priority to either technological innovation or advance in intelligence as the basis for human "progress." It should be noted, nonetheless, that in expressing the hope that the machine might condition the masses to matter-of-fact thinking Becker *did* lean somewhat away from his stated position of neutrality on this matter.

Of course, in our time, the focus of interest in a technological cultural cure has moved away from television, McLuhan's hope of the 1960s, to the computer and all the startling possibilities which the latter now offers. It is this technology which occupies center stage at the present time, though it appears that initial enthusiasm for its revolutionary role, at least in education, has begun to wane—if only a little. An MIT mathematician and educational philosopher, Seymour Papert, originator of the Logo computer program, best expressed that hope in his 1980 book *Mindstorms: Children, Computers, and Powerful Ideas.* The book became required reading for school administrators across the nation as computer companies sought to establish the educational (and household) necessity of their product. Papert's project for programming children to think mathematically has received wide support from the business community, caught up in worldwide technological competition, but Papert also saw his Logo program (and the computer) as a means to personal development and personal power. Papert says, "A central idea behind our learning environments was that children would be able to use powerful ideas from mathematics and science as instruments of personal power."[58] Subsequent classroom experience and educational second thoughts have moderated expectations on this point and voices of concern, such as Sherry Turkle's *The Second Self: Computers and the Human Spirit,*[59] are also now being heard. Thus expressions of hope centered in machine technology—as Becker himself expressed that hope—continue to be heard and will likely continue to be voiced. Many people apparently will continue to view this as a better hope than the political—a more manageable one.

Becker's third hope, that society might experience some respite from technological innovation, is, from the present perspective, the most illusory. Technological innovation continues to accelerate and there is no thought or suggestion of its slackening its pace. Society continues to suffer the dislocation and turmoil which new technologies bring. Job loss through automation, the export of industrial production overseas, new pressures on the educational systems, an increasing competitiveness across all levels of society, a growing sense of the temporary nature of human relationships: these patterns continue to engulf an ever-larger number of the population at large. Technological innovation itself, directly and indirectly, increasingly defines the political agenda not only for the United States but for all industrialized nations—and manifestly also the Soviet Union.

It is often—most commonly—argued that technology is neutral, that it is only a tool. This argument is frequently put forth by those most deeply involved in, and most committed to, the furtherance of technology. The historical evidence, however, weighs against the neutrality of technology—and this is graphically illustrated by the futility of Becker's third hope, the forlorn thought of a stay in technological innovation, which would enable society to recover and assimilate the changes that have already occurred. Clearly the rate of technological innovation has not slackened, it has only continued to accelerate. The great historical truth of our time is that there seems to be little that can be done to check its rapid worldwide spread.

In a provocative 1977 study of this theme,[60] Langdon Winner offered the testimony of respected cultural observers on the matter. A listing of a few of their assessments suggests that such concern is neither isolated nor idiosyncratic: John Kenneth Galbraith: "I am led to the conclusion . . . that we are becoming the servants in thought as in action, of the machine we have created to serve us"; René Dubos: "Technology cannot theoretically escape from human control, but in practice it is proceeding on an essentially independent course"; Martin Heidegger: "No one can foresee the radical changes to come. But technological advance will move faster and faster and can never be stopped. In all areas of his existence, man will be encircled ever more tightly by the forces of technology—these forces—have moved long since beyond his will and have outgrown his capacity for decision."[61] Werner Heisenberg, Paul Valéry, Herbert Marcuse, Jacques Ellul, Lewis Mumford, the list of those who have addressed the question of "technics-out-of-control" goes on. It seems that one must speak here in biblical-theological terms of a "principality" or "power," a ruling force in the lives of people which captivates and claims, usurps the control it was supposed to provide.

While others like Ellul and Winner have provided analysis of the phenomenon of "technique," the drive for mastery and efficiency in production and organization, our own description of technology's rise, against the backdrop of the idea of Progress, provides perhaps a better clue to its power over us. Technology speaks to us out of a profound disillusion with the great political hope which helped inspire the original belief in Progress—the idea that by eliminating ignorance and a corrupt social order, humanity could accomplish its own fulfillment. Technology now provides a lesser hope. Its promise is concrete but also vague, without demand for conscious sacrifice. Thus the disillusion which it breeds is less acute. It offers something of a distraction from the earlier hope, the desire for a deepened belonging within the framework of human community. Technology's distractions are short-lived: a new style, a new design, a new convenience, the passage of some time and then boredom, and the search for something new. Sometimes the vision of a new technology revivifies briefly the old political hope, the hope of deliverance, if not a perfection: the computer and a Seymour Papert, a "third wave" and an Alvin Toffler.[62] But with the passage of five or six years, the excitement, the stir, the resolve are gone, and we wait for something new. Technology will provide this and we forget the promises with which the last technology came.

Something also is found in technology—something more basic than distraction—that which technology is and always was: power. Becker so described it. Power can be its own end, without political-social purpose. When Machiavelli published *The Prince* in 1513, power was still defined in terms of political structure; the pursuit of power was essentially a political game. Later, technology, in league with capitalism, very much broadened the scope of the power quest. Once more Becker illumines and informs. He remarks that the old order of kings and priests yielded—in major part—to "technological appliances and the symbols of fluid wealth."[63] By "symbols of fluid wealth" Becker meant money capital, in contrast to land and class. Such symbols meant a bourgeois culture in succession to a feudal one. It meant limited liability and the legal definition of corporations. It also meant patent law, the legal protection of invention and the assurance of profitability.

In many textbooks on the history of technology one does not read a great deal about the origins of patent law, or its impact upon the subsequent course of technological innovation. There were early forms of patent law in fifteenth-century Florence and Venice, but the English patent law of 1623 set the pattern for most subsequent national patent systems.[64] Lewis Mumford, in his *Technics and Civilization*, draws a contrast between what had existed earlier with the craft guilds and what came into existence with the establishment of patent law. Mumford comments:

> The tendency of organization by crafts [A.D. 900–1400] regulated in the interests of standardized and efficient work, guaranteed by local monopolies, was on the whole conservative. In the beginning, it was knowledge,

skill, experience, that had been the subjects of guild monopoly. With the growth of capitalism came the bestowing of special monopolies, first to the chartered companies, and then to the owners of special patents granted for specific original inventions. This was proposed by Bacon in 1601 and happened first in England in 1624 [1623]. From this time on it *was not the past heritage that was effectively monopolized but the new departure from it.*[65]

Mumford's emphasis here accents an equivalent in economics and technology to what has been argued above[66] in relation to knowledge and politics and the changed attitude toward change so fundamental in the rise of the belief in Progress. What it secured was a new form of power available to the inventive and commercial mind, helping to establish also the new class of the entrepreneur and the merchant. Continuous innovation, not conservation, is the source of power in the world that has emerged since the seventeenth century; and technology by assuring always some new conquest of power is itself the engine that drives the machine of modern society.

Here, however, some reassessment is urgently needed. A technological and economic system has been legislated—it is not simply a "natural development"[67]—which both promises economic, social, political power to those who seek it and continually generates new power. The accumulation of power in all its forms, social, economic, political, physical (Becker's "sources of power"), has exceeded any clearly defined social purpose and threatens not only the international political order but the ecosystem as well. We speak here not only of a nuclear holocaust but possibly of billions of apparently insignificant chlorofluorocarbon spray containers, innumerable refrigeration units, and vast amounts of Styrofoam insulation distributed indiscriminately across the world. To ease the economic hurt of an immediate halt of the production of chlorofluorocarbons an international agreement was reached to cap production at 1986 levels in 1990 and then reduce production to one half in the following "several years." A major U.S. newspaper, in an editorial, commented on the agreement: "The plan offers welcome evidence that other nations recognize the threat to the ozone shield and will sacrifice to preserve it."[68] There has to be some irony in the use of the word "sacrifice" in this context. The sacrifice is cessation of damage to the environment and to unnumbered human and animal lives. In describing the phenomenon of "technological drift," Langdon Winner writes:

> A multiplicity of technologies, developed and applied under a very narrow range of considerations, act and interact in countless ways beyond the anticipations of any person or institution. Except in cases of extreme danger or disaster, there are almost no existing means of controlling or regu-

lating the products of this chain of events. . . . As the speed and extent of technological innovation increase, societies face the distinct possibility of going adrift in a vast sea of "unintended consequences."[69]

What then has become of Progress when the only form in which we have it is technology? Whither does the pursuit of power lead when it is no longer centered in a stated social goal?[70] We address such questions in the next chapter, "Technology and Values."

4

TECHNOLOGY
AND VALUES

In the aftermath of the dropping of the atomic bombs in 1945, the scientific community underwent a troubled soul-searching. The scientific director of the Manhattan Project Robert Oppenheimer declared forthrightly, "The physicists have known sin." Who better to speak such words than the one whose theoretical expertise and organizational genius had seen the construction of the bomb through to its successful test at Alamogordo, New Mexico, and then its first use over Hiroshima? In Europe a group of German scientists who had made contributions to the development of nuclear physics were similarly affected. Werner Heisenberg has described the impact of the first news of the Hiroshima bombing upon his colleagues.

> Worst hit of all was Otto Hahn. Uranium fission, his most important scientific discovery, had been the crucial step on the road toward atomic power. And this step had now led to the horrible destruction of a large city and its population, of a host of unarmed and mostly innocent people. Hahn withdrew to his room visibly shaken and deeply disturbed, and all of us were afraid that he might do himself some injury.[1]

Though a sense of guilt was widespread among the scientific community, it did not by any means represent a uniform response. Carl Friedrich von Weiszacker denied that any scientist doing pure research could be held responsible for its technological application.[2] Heisenberg argued that there is an ineluctable quality to the course of scientific inquiry and that the general course of such research was more decisive than any individual's single contribution.[3]

In America, many who shared in the building of the bomb, rejected Oppenheimer's confession of guilt, pointing to the bomb's effective termination of the war. An especially interesting disclaimer of scientific culpability was provided by the physicist Jacob Bronowski. In a series of lectures at the Massachusetts Institute of Technology in 1953, Bronowski gave account of his own struggles with the question of scientific guilt. Soon after the war with Japan had ended, Bronowski was sent to Nagasaki to help appraise the damage caused by the bomb. He tells of arriving in Nagasaki late at night and searching out his quarters on a U.S. Navy ship moored in the harbor. In approaching the ship in the dark, he describes hearing a then current hit song being played over the ship's public-address system, "Is You Is Or Is You Ain't My Baby?" Bronowski's judgment was that the bomb was *not* science's "baby." Whereas Von Weiszacker had argued that the bomb was the responsibility of the physicists, not in their role as scientists but only in their role as inventors/technicians, Bronowski argued that the bomb was the work of society as a whole and that the ruins of Nagasaki were testimony to the failure of society's values and not those of science.[4]

Bronowski, in sum, offers an apologetic for science, arguing that the most crucial values for modern civilization are rooted in the practice of science. Strongly inclined also to the positive values of the arts, Bronowski argued for the common nature of creative achievement in both science and the arts; but he was primarily concerned to make the case that the cherished values of independence, originality, and dissent were chiefly rooted in the practice of science. Bronowski declared:

> The society of scientists is simple because it has a directing purpose: to explore the truth. Nevertheless, it has to solve the problem of every society which is to find a compromise between man and men. It must encourage the single scientist to be independent and the body of scientists to be tolerant. From these basic conditions, which form the prime values, there follows step by step a range of values: dissent, freedom of thought and speech, justice, honor, human dignity and self-respect.[5]

Bronowski goes on to conclude: "The dilemma of today is not that the human values cannot control a mechanical science. It is the other way about; the scientific spirit is more human than the machinery of governments. . . . Our conduct as states clings to a code of self interest which science, like humanity, has long left behind."[6]

In a 1956 preface to the revised edition of his lectures Bronowski draws back a little from his earlier declaration that the practice of science establishes "the prime values" of civilization. The lectures were allowed to stand as they were delivered; but he notes in the later preface that what he had originally argued was that science yields "a fundamental set of universal values," *not* "that this set embraces all the human values."[7] He later allowed that there were some values such as tenderness, kindness, and love which are not generated by science. Still, he reaffirmed the burden of his original argument that governments are chiefly to blame for the modern-day moral crisis, that they are far less moral than the community of scientists.

Here, however, it must be pointed out, against Bronowski, that it was precisely the breakdown of trust within the scientific community that led to the building of the bomb in the first place. Certainly Bronowski's statement of the unifying ethos of the scientific community is exaggerated, and it lacks the critical perspective of more recent studies in the sociology of science, studies which point up the fierce competitiveness of the scientific enterprise.[8]

An additional point at issue in Bronowski's analysis is his conflation of science and technology. In this he represents a minority viewpoint among philosophers of science.[9] He writes: "I define science as the organization of our knowledge in such a way that it commands more of the hidden potential in nature. What I have in mind therefore is both deep and matter of fact; it reaches from the kinetic theory of gases to the telephone and the suspension bridge and medicated tooth paste. It admits no sharp boundary between knowledge and use."[10] Certainly Von Weiszacker's distinction between the researcher and the inventor does not hold here, nor does the important distinction between the purpose of understanding (science) and that of control (technology).

There are sound theoretical and analytical grounds for rejecting Bronowski's marriage of science and technology, but the historical reasons for doing so seem compelling. The history of technology in the West, up through much of the nineteenth century, was primarily that of "empirical technology," a technology deriving from practical, cumulative improvements, the result of inventive genius, but not deriving from a theoretical, scientific knowledge. A historian of technology, D. S. L. Cardwell, in his *Turning Points in Western Technology,* structures much of his history upon this distinction. In describing the onset of the Industrial Revolution in the latter half of the eighteenth century, Cardwell writes: "The invention of textile machinery by men like Arkwright, Hargraves, Coniah Wood, Crompton, and many others was totally independent of science. It is true that the mechanical philosophy may have had some very general and indirect influence on the process of invention in the textile field but to all intents and purposes these inventions belong to the category that we have designated empirical and non-science based."[11]

This distinction figures large in the debates over the role of science in the Industrial Revolution, with most historians suggesting an important role for a science-based technology only in the Industrial Revolution's later stages, especially in the dyeing and textile-processing industries (chemistry).[12] Certainly science-based technology played only a minor role later on in World War I (poison gas) compared to its major role in World War II (radar, jet aircraft engine, ballistic missiles, but especially the atomic bomb). As we have suggested, it was the scientific community's involvement in the technology of nuclear power that precipitated the whole discussion of science and values.[13]

If at an earlier time science served as a psychologically liberating force, providing Western society with much of its early self-confidence,[14] in the aftermath of World War II it can be argued that it became a source of increased anxiety. Less visible than science but more immediate in its impact, technology has come in our time to play the dominant role. It promises less, but delivers more. Science, like politics, has increasingly fallen under the sway of technology. The function of science in Western society is now less spiritual than practical, less a matter of understanding than of power. Though still motivated by curiosity, science has increasingly become the servant of technology.

Important in this assessment of the decline of science vis-à-vis technology is the perception that the scientific community is much more identifiable and thus more responsible than the community of those involved in technological innovation. The diffuse character of technological decision making, spread across the corporate-management structure, the anonymity of the technicians themselves, the team character of their work,[15] make the technological enterprise and its social responsibilities more difficult to fix. Individuals seem to achieve public notice in the technical field most frequently when something goes wrong—as in the Challenger disaster or Chernobyl. Occasionally individuals emerge out of the corporate-technological network to blow the whistle, calling attention to corporate-bureaucratic malfeasance or an environmental abuse. But the community responsible for technological innovation is certainly much more divided in purpose, much more disparate, than that involved in scientific research. Also, it can be said that the general public, in its consumptive appetite, is much more involved in technological advance. Technology offers always some new immediacy, some new luxury, along with relief from the boredom of past technologies. The people who do technology most frequently simply assume they are fulfilling society's values: extending life, easing the burden of work, providing new comforts and diversions, and simply solving problems. Some others—such as corporate managers—understand technology to be a vital means of securing economic power, a necessity in economic competition. Others, in government, see it as an essential means of military and international power.

One cannot so nicely derive a set of values from the "community" of technology as Bronowski believed he was able to do for the community of science. It would be difficult to claim for technology such a range of values as "dissent, freedom of thought and speech, justice, honor, human dignity and self-respect," though it is conceivable that someone may yet undertake such an effort. Nevertheless the history of technology is of such long duration and so culturally varied in its past expressions that the derivation of a specific set of values from its practice would seem to be difficult to achieve. For example, the explanation usually given for the failure of technological expansion in ancient Chinese culture—or in Greek culture—is that the dominant values of those cultures simply did not support such expansion. One often hears that because the Romans condoned slavery and rejected a universal human dignity there was small need for laborsaving technology or that the particular values which dominated the ruling elite among the Romans—and the Greeks—simply did not direct attention to the technological possibility. If technology were a cohesive, formative force in the shaping of social values, why did those groups most involved in the technical arts fail to participate in the ferment of political and social change, fail to see themselves as the vanguard of a new, more humane society rather than as subjects of imperial and class patronage?

In his argument on behalf of science and technology as the bearers of the essential human values, Bronowski states, "Those who crusade against the rational, and receive their values by mystic inspiration have no claim to these values of the mind."[16] Once more, I have argued that one *has* to leave room for "mystic inspiration"—for the religious tradition—as a factor in the framing of many of society's basic values. Thus, in attempting to explain the peculiar acceleration of technological progress during the Middle Ages, the historian Lynn White, Jr., makes the suggestion that because Christianity valued physical labor as a spiritual discipline it came also to distinguish between a humane and a dehumanizing labor. White writes:

> The monks of the first millennium both in the Greek East and the Latin West worked as a form of worship. In doing so they defied the classical attitude towards manual labor which continued to be sustained by the aristocratic society which was their context. So great was the general respect for the laboring monk that we can scarcely escape the conclusion that the attitudes of peasants and artisans towards their own labors, and towards the moral value of labor, were improved. Here we can identify . . . [a] post-Roman psychic innovation favorable to the vigorous expansion of technology. . . . In late Antiquity, with rare exceptions, learned men did not work, and workers were not learned. The monks were the first large group of intellectuals to get dirt under their fingernails: surely a fact related to the growth of technology.[17]

Again White asserts:

Until the fourth century, the Jewish heresy called Christianity remained largely a proletarian faith. By proclaiming that (as St. Peter put it) "God is no respecter of persons" (Acts X:34) the new religion gave dignity to the humble, and, by implication, to their banausic activities.[18]

What White argues, contra Bronowski, is that religion had a vital role to play in nurturing the surge of technological invention and its widespread dissemination during the Middle Ages. White, however, is not entirely clear on whether these formative religious values were necessary to sustain technology after it gained momentum; he argues only that they played an indispensable role in fostering technological innovation at a critical point in its historical development. While there are aspects of White's analysis that are similar to Max Weber's argument regarding Calvinism and the rise of capitalism, White is silent on whether, once established as a historical force, technology, like capitalism, continued its expansion independent of the religious values that helped nurture it.[19]

Because of the diffuse nature of the technological community and technology's diverse history, it is not likely, as we have suggested, that one will argue successfully for a special set of values deriving from the practice of technological invention which, in the past, have proved essential to society. Such an argument would also, of course, run counter to the widespread view that technology is basically a neutral phenomenon, that tools are value-free. Yet there are those who bear the technological commitment—and some historians as well—who press beyond this viewpoint of technological neutrality and, while not endorsing the idea of a comprehensive set of social values, nonetheless propose that technology has served in some special way the basic values of freedom and democracy, freedom and equality.

This is an interesting and seemingly more credible viewpoint. Its roots can be traced, with some justification, back to Francis Bacon (1561–1626), who early saw the potential for change in science and the practical arts. Though not convinced of the Copernican cosmology, Bacon was much impressed with the growth of new knowledge accruing from the revolution in navigation (the compass) and disseminated by the printing press. As the Lord Chancellor of England under James I, Bacon was also politically concerned for stability and he was a strong supporter of the monarchy. He saw, however, that change was the order of the day. Bacon's question was How was this change to be accomplished without accentuating religious and political turmoil? He eventually described a program in which science and technology, not religion—a science and technology ordered and encouraged by the state, the monarchy and parliament—was to serve as the chief means of advancing the social order. Bacon scorned aspects of the old order, especially the speculative propensities of scholasticism, and the philosophical heritage of Platonism and Aristotelianism. Bacon had a sense for "entrenched interest," at least in the intellectual sphere, and countered it by affirming a movement from cloister to the world parallel to that which inspired Luther's religious reform, but which was centered instead on technology. In his *Advancement of Learning* (1605), Bacon writes:

> Another error hath proceeded from too great a reverence, and a kind of adoration of the mind and understanding of man, by means whereof, men have withdrawn themselves too much from the contemplation of nature and the observations of experience, and have trembled up and down in their own reason and conceits. Upon these intellectualists, which are notwithstanding commonly taken for the most sublime and divine philosophers, Heraclitus gave a just censure, saying, "Men sought truth in their own little worlds and not in the great and common world"; for they disdain to spell, and so by degrees to read in the volume of God's works: and contrariwise by continual meditation and agitation of wit do urge and as it were invocate their own spirits to divine and give oracles unto them, whereby they are deservedly deluded.[20]

In affirming "the great and common world" in contrast to the innumerable speculative worlds of the philosophers and schoolmen, Bacon argued for the empirical method and the practical arts. This was a sphere, he felt, open to people of the common sort. In the *Novum Organum* he writes, "But the course I propose for the discovery of sciences is such as leaves but little to the acuteness and strength of wits, but places all wits and understanding nearly on a level."[21] These egalitarian sentiments, however, did not entail political criticism, rather, they envisioned only the systematizing of the method of invention, sponsored by the state.[22] Bacon's program clearly aimed at the welfare of the "commonwealth," and addressed the needs of the common people. In this sense he expressed a humanly inclusive, a "democratic" purpose. Bacon saw all of this, with the exception of the universities and their monopoly of knowledge, structured on the basis of the old political order. Freedom as such was not the goal, but knowledge and human betterment were. Both national loyalty and a limited egalitarian commitment inspired Bacon's vision of the future. He was concerned for "the great and common world" and rejected simultaneously a privileged, intellectual elite. Heraclitus provided Bacon with the quotation on "the great and common world" but the egalitarian motif suggests affinities with the religious ethos.[23] Bacon's commitment to the practical arts (technology) is perhaps best understood as a form of the earlier commitment to a "priesthood of all believers," but limited to the acquisition of a new and practical knowledge.

One can say that Bacon's political philosophy was more informed by Luther than Calvin in his acceptance of the established political order. He did not criticize that order so much as he sought to work for "new life" within it.[24] The Calvinist and Puritan perspective, by contrast, was much more critical of the established political, ecclesiastical structures and more prone to radical revision. It was, in short, much more revolutionary in intent and spirit.[25] In our time, with the flagging of political hope and zeal, Bacon's project of empiricism and his suggestion that "truth" is largely defined by innovation and the practical arts appear more in keeping with the current mood and temper. One can say that his analysis and projected program fit well with the post-Enlightenment, post-revolutionary disillusion with the political possibility, all of which we have discussed in chapter 3 above in relation to Carl Becker. In the *Novum Organum* Bacon writes, "Truths therefore and utility are here the very same things: and works themselves are of greater value as pledges of truth."[26]

Clearly, in the twentieth-century world, God is no longer looked to as the source of human dignity and worth—not substantively, in the culture at large; nor are the values of freedom and equality grounded in bold sweeping philosophical declarations, in a doctrine of "natural rights" as in the eighteenth century. Rather, in the twentieth century, freedom and equality, the values of democracy, are increasingly viewed as somehow natural emergents out of a long historical process; and, by some, they are claimed to be offshoots of the history of technological advance.

Toward the end of the nineteenth century, when some people like Henry Adams and William Dean Howells were expressing doubts about the course of technological development, others dedicated to that same development began to see in particular technological innovations the furtherance if not the source of democratic values. Thus, in 1892, Charles H. Loring, an engineer, "argued that the steam engine had made it possible for man to abolish slavery and had opened up vistas for future progress undreamed of by the ancients."[27] Other forms of the same argument have surfaced throughout the twentieth century. In 1948, a British historian of technology, Samuel Lilley, declared iron to be the "democratic metal." Bronze, Lilley argued,

> had implied the centralization of economic power, and therefore also a political power in the hands of an aristocratic few. Iron, with its consequence of good tools and weapons for a much greater number, and with

the large classes of craftsmen and traders, independent of the patronage of noble families, led to a greater economic equality and a decentralization of economic power. Inevitably, this must produce political changes of a corresponding nature. The first centuries of the Iron Age show a gradual democratization of society (not without bitter resistance from the aristocrats) till by 450 B.C. Athens had a constitution in which there were virtually no legal differences between the rights of *citizens*.[28]

Lilley notes that "the word 'citizens' is italicized because this democracy was limited by the exclusion of women, slaves, and foreigners from citizenship."[29] And he went on to assert that democratization of the classical world did not progress further because the institution of slavery stood in the way, to be removed later, in Loring's view, by the development of the steam engine.

As recently as 1973 a similar argument surfaced in a *Scientific American* article on "Bicycle Technology." The author, S. S. Wilson, declared that in the early 1880s, after Queen Victoria ordered two Royal Salvo tricycles for her personal use, respectability was won for "the new craze of cycling. It made it possible for well-brought up young ladies to get out and away from the stuffiness of their Victorian homes and led to such new freedoms as 'rational dress,' a trend led by Amelia Jenks Bloomer. It is not too farfetched to suggest that the coincidence of cycling with the gradual spread of education for women played a significant part in the early stages of women's movement toward political and economic equality."[30] Similar arguments have been made for the role of the automobile and the radio in fostering freedoms essential to a democratic society.

Most recently it is the computer which has been proposed as the instrument for enhancing democratic freedom. In 1974, a political scientist, Hazel Henderson, argued that the computer would have the effect of stimulating the growth of new interest groups by overcoming chronic deficiencies in organization.[31] It was also predicted that computers would provide greater checks and more efficient input from the voting constituency. Such suggestions were subsequently taken up and popularized by Alvin Toffler in his 1980 best-seller *The Third Wave*. Toffler argued—in a popular, journalistic style—that all of our current political institutions have been outdated by the new (the third) wave of information-processing technology. We have entered "the post-industrial age" (Daniel Bell's phrase) and now the new structures of political governance must be redesigned to make room for the spread of issue-oriented interest groups and the potentialities of the computer for expanding the role of direct, plebiscite-structured democracy in contrast to the "representative form" characteristic of the passing industrial era (the "second wave"). More than half of Toffler's short-term (fifteen- to twenty-year) future has transpired since he wrote his best-seller and already the glitter has faded on his vision of the "democratic computer" and its social-political role. Sober critics of the democratic computer suggest that economic-political elites have used the computer to maintain their positions of power and the control of information.[32] And one observer sees, contra Toffler, "a trend away from direct political participation in decision-making toward more expertly controlled political structures."[33] A review of international economic developments since Toffler published his *Third Wave* suggests no breakup of traditional structures of power, but rather the continued centralization of power in the larger economic-corporate enterprises. It is also interesting to note that those industrialized nations which can claim a strong ethnic identity (e.g., Japan, Germany) seem better equipped to compete for economic power in world markets[34] than the less disciplined, less cohesive societies.

This effort to claim "democratic" significance for particular technologies has also been accompanied, most recently, by an attempt to ascribe democratic significance to the whole phenomenon of technological innovation and expansion. In the aftermath of the American Bicentennial celebration Daniel J. Boorstin, the respected historian and Librarian of Congress, published a collection of essays entitled *The Republic of Technology: Reflections of Our Future Community.* In this little book, Boorstin celebrated the union of technology and politics in "the American Experiment." After starting off with a delineation of what can be regarded as the major differences between technological and political change, Boorstin counters by arguing that what is in fact distinctive about American political history is that it embraces and confirms the major operative characteristics of technology.

Boorstin sets out his argument in the following manner:

> If we look back, then, on the great political revolutions and the great technological revolutions (both of which are clues to the range of mankind's capacities and possibilities) we see a striking contrast. Political revolutions, generally speaking, have revealed man's organized purposefulness, his social conscience, his sense of justice—the aggressive, assertive side of his nature. Technological change, invention, and innovation have tended rather to reveal his play instinct, his desire and his ability to go where he has never gone, to do what he has never done. The one shows his willingness to sacrifice in order to fulfill his plans, the other his willingness to sacrifice in order to pursue his quest.[35]

Boorstin adds a further word to this distinction. Political revolutions, he says, are "displacive": the new political order takes the place of the old, overthrows it. But revolutions are also reversible: one can have a counterrevolution, and the old order can be restored. "In the political world, you can go home again."[36] By contrast, Boorstin asserts that advances in technology do not simply replace older technologies as much as they encourage the definition of new functions for the earlier technologies.[37] The telephone did not make the postman obsolete nor did television mark the death of the radio—or the book. Thus the history of technology, according to Boorstin, is characterized more by reordering than by displacement. It is also characterized by irreversibility, in contrast to the possibility of restoration in politics. Nothing ever gets "uninvented" in the history of technology. And while it is possible to conceive of alternatives to modernity, private Waldens embraced by the few, these retreats serve only as reminders "that the march of modernity is ruthless" and cannot be stayed.[38]

A final difference between technology and politics mentioned by Boorstin is the limitless possibilities of technological invention versus the very restricted set of political options that confront the politically thoughtful citizen. Whereas in technology one dare not dogmatically state that such and such is impossible, in politics utopian dreams are very much on the decline. Boorstin cites two laws, one for each of the two histories. In technology the law can be stated in the following terms: "When a distinguished but elderly scientist states that something is possible, he is most certainly right. When he states that something is impossible, he is very probably wrong." In politics the law runs simply as follows: "Political wisdom does not substantially progress."[39]

Having described these contrasting differences between technology and politics, Boorstin then proceeds in the remainder of his book to bring about their reconciliation—on American soil, and by means of his own interpretation of the purposes of the Founding Fathers and the Constitution. The sum of this interpretation is that the Founders were not so much political ideologues as simple pragmatists, experimenters in the form of government, the bearers of a "technological spirit."[40] Not inclined to foreclose the future, the Founding Fathers, according to Boorstin, sought to design a government open to the future and its unforeseen possibilities. The phrase "We, the people . . . ," which introduces the Constitution, was itself open to new interpretations, new inclusions. Boorstin comments:

> The framers had the wisdom, in preparing a Constitution for posterity, not to try to elaborate or make more explicit the meaning of "the people," they did not say "we the property owners" or "we the qualified voters." Their words, an adequate working definition in their time, would be a providential receptacle for new meanings—as civil and political rights

were extended to non-property owners, to former slaves, to women, to persons above the age of eighteen, and possibly to other categories now still beyond our imagining.[41]

In similar spirit, the framers left open the Constitution to amendment and the future inclusion of new member states within the Union. "The Founding Fathers," Boorstin argues, "declared themselves custodians of an expanding future. Federalism was their grand device for holding together experimenting communities. . . . The ingenious Add-a-State Plan allowed a national laboratory to grow by installments." In all of this "experimentation" Boorstin sees a consonance between the political project and technology. He says: "What federalism was in the world of politics, technology would be in the minutiae of everyday life. While ideology 'fenced in,' federalism—and technology—tried out. Just as federalism would test still-unexplored possibilities in government, so technology would test unimagined possibilities in the modes of common experience."[42]

Boorstin's ringing declaration of confidence in "the republic of technology" captures well some of the spirit of the 1976 American Bicentennial, for it not only celebrates a past but proclaims a confident future. By joining the nation to that power in the modern world which does not look back, Boorstin seemingly assures the nation its next two hundred years. His tour de force, however, leaves many questions, many doubts—some certainly that arise out of the more than ten years that have passed since he wrote. The American people would seem, in the light of these past few years, to have no inborn "technological spirit," none, at least, which would guarantee the republic against the ascending power of other peoples with less commitment to the democratic ethos. Boorstin's argument infers that the "spirit of technology," the innocent spirit of adventure and novelty, empiricism and "experimentation," can carry the democratic commitment.

In contrast to Boorstin's "enthusiasm" John Kasson's analysis of the American experience with technology is much more sober and soul-searching. Kasson's account, discussed in chapter 2 above, speaks of an American effort to "civilize the machine." It describes a deep-rooted conflict between "technology and republican values" and an ongoing struggle, not an easy coalescence. The two books, the one by Boorstin and the other by Kasson, overlap in the time of their publication but not in their history. The thoughtful reader is called to decide which history is "true," which history properly describes the American—and the human—situation.[43]

Boorstin's assertion of the common ground of technological and democratic values, independent of his historical argument, reflects a widespread and growing technological rationalization of the democratic commitment. The argument simply put is that technology demands freedom, or a certain measure of freedom, for its proper functioning. Technology, it is suggested—and fairly so—demands creativity and interchange, and this, it is argued, happens more readily within the framework of a spontaneous and free society than within a controlled one, within a capitalistic than within a socialistic economic order. One can, in this last decade of the twentieth century, survey the changes that are sweeping the two great, controlled political orders, the U.S.S.R. and China, and argue that the moves toward liberalization are dictated by the necessities of economic and technological competition, that a certain measure of freedom is essential to the furtherance of technological innovation and power. Here it is also possible to argue that only that measure of freedom need be allowed which can sustain the efficient functioning of the technological system. Freedom and equality, the chief democratic values, are here made conditional, assimilated to a manageable system, with inputs and outputs, controlled and manipulated by a ruling or "expert" elite which understands the necessities of technology and power. Boorstin might hail this non-"ideological" possibility—as might also B. F. Skinner. It does not, however, speak to the question of human dignity, a question very much at issue in the founding of the American republic.

One final viewpoint needs discussion in this survey of the question of technology and democratic values. This is the somber view of the cultural historian and city planner Lewis Mumford. Mumford does not see in the history of technology a step-by-step enlargement of human freedom such as that proposed by the advocates of "democratic" metals, or steam engines, or computers; nor does he see in the whole process of technological innovation some guarantee, or warrant, for human freedom. Rather, Mumford maintains that throughout the course of civilization there is manifest a continuing struggle between two types of technology: one democratic and the other authoritarian and enslaving.

There were intimations of this point of view in Mumford's early major work *Technics and Civilization* (1934)[44]; but it is in *The Myth of the Machine: Technics and Human Development* (1966) that Mumford articulates most clearly his argument for an ages-long struggle between two kinds of technology: one patterned on the building of the pyramids in Egypt and the other on the seemingly lesser skills of artistic creation, one oriented toward power and the other toward aesthetic satisfaction. Mumford writes, "At its point of origin, technics was related to the whole nature of man, and that nature played a part in every aspect of industry: thus technics, at the beginning, was broadly life-centered, not work-centered or power-centered."[45] With the so-called "rise of civilization" during the fourth millennium B.C.E. a new form of social organization came into being which, claiming the sanction of a cosmic order, was able to reduce the craftsman to the role of a mere component. "By a combination of divine command and ruthless military coercion, a large population was made to endure grinding poverty and forced labor at mind-dulling repetitive tasks in order to ensure 'life, prosperity, and health' for the divine or semi-divine ruler and his entourage." Mumford argues that "conceptually the instruments of mechanization five thousand years ago were already detached from other human functions and purposes and were directed at the constant increase of order, power, predictability, and above all, control. With this proto-scientific ideology went a corresponding regimentation and degradation of once-autonomous human activities: 'mass culture' and 'mass control' made their first appearance."[46]

Elsewhere Mumford writes:

> What I call democratic technics is the small scale method of production, resting mainly on human skill and animal energy but always, even when employing machines, remaining under the active direction of the craftsman or the farmer, each group developing its own gifts, through appropriate arts and social ceremonies, as well as making discreet use of the gifts of nature. . . . This democratic technics has underpinned and firmly supported every historic culture until our own day, and redeemed the constant tendency of authoritarian technics to misapply its powers. Even when paying tribute to the most oppressive authoritarian regimes, there yet remained within the workshop or the farmyard some degree of autonomy, selectivity, creativity. No royal mace, no slave-driver's whip, no bureaucratic directive left its imprint on the textiles of Damascus or the pottery of fifth century Athens.[47]

This democratic technics was associated with the earliest forms of culture and the early use of tools. Then came the later institutions of monarchy and the bureaucratic structuring of society. The Egyptians were the recognized ancient masters of this art. Claiming to be the embodiment of divine and cosmic powers the pharaohs mobilized armies for work, armies for war, armies for political-social control (bureaucracy). With these instruments they succeeded in constructing huge private and public works (the pyramids, irrigation systems, canals) which utilized "thousands of horsepower centuries before horses were harnessed or wheels invented."[48] Such authoritarian technics provided a new abundance in food supply, led to the development of large urban centers, and provided a high degree of specialization. But it was not—nor is it today in its modern form—capable of fulfilling the deepest needs of human self-expression and fulfillment, for it demands too great a surrender to "the mechanical collective." The modern authoritarian technics, of course, no longer claim a personal, divine sanction. Mumford writes:

> The center of authority in this new system is no longer a visible personality, an all powerful king: even in totalitarian dictatorships the center now lies in the system itself, invisible but omnipresent; all its human components, even the technical and managerial elite, even the sacred priesthood of science, who alone have access to the secret knowledge by means of which total control is now swiftly being effected, are themselves trapped by the very perfection of the organization they have invented. Their praise of the system is an act of self-worship. . . . They are in the grip of an irrational compulsion to extend their means of control and expand the scope of their authority. . . . The ultimate end of this technics is to displace life, or rather, to transfer the attributes of life to the machine and the mechanical collective.[49]

Mumford is far from sanguine about the ability of democratic technics to withstand the onslaught of the modern form of authoritarian technics. He offers only a warning that surrender to this form of modern technology may mean the surrender of that which is most distinctively human. "Life," he declares, "cannot be delegated."[50]

Beyond question, Boorstin and Mumford provide two very different readings of the democratic nature—and hope—of technology. They certainly have moved the question of technology and democratic values beyond the simplistic identification of these values with particular technologies (e.g., the printing press, the steam engine, the computer) to a consideration of the phenomenon of technology itself and how it operates in our present world. Boorstin offers a very benign view of technology as essentially "experimental and open-ended," "adventurous and questful," whereas Mumford is deeply concerned with what he views as technology's preoccupation with power and control. For Mumford, local community, the crafts, and artistic expression are the guarantors of what is most distinctively human and fulfilling. However, even with Mumford's humane and caring concern for art, symbol, and small-group identity, we may not have come to the nub of the matter, the question of what is threatened by technology and how it has come to command so much of the life we now live.

Here let us suggest that an important dimension of what freedom and equality mean, what democracy at its best seeks to preserve, is uniquely expressed in the thought of Martin Buber in his classic work *I and Thou.* Already by 1923, as indicated in the preceding discussion, questions about technology had often been raised on both sides of the Atlantic. In America the questions centered on technology's role in enhancing or diminishing democratic values as these had been expressed within the framework of an agrarian society. In Europe, they centered more directly on technology's potential threat to human selfhood, and it is this latter question which Buber perceptively addressed in his *I and Thou.*

The fundamental thesis of Buber's work is that the individual, the human person, is related to the world in two ways, that of "the primary word I-Thou" and that of "the primary word I-It." The human self, the "I," is "two-fold."[51] When the self relates impersonally to the world, when things in the world serve as mere objects, the "I" gives expression to the I-It relationship. Here the self—as it must in order to survive—is concerned to pursue goals and objectives. It is concerned to control and manipulate, to treat the world, things, and people, as a means of satisfying personal needs and desires. Everyone in some important measure relates to the world in this manner.

Buber goes on to assert that relating solely to the world and to "others" in this manner is to fail of one's basic humanity, for the one "who lives with *It* alone is not a man." To realize fully one's selfhood one must enter into a relationship with a "Thou," another person. Buber says: "If I face a human being as my *Thou,* and say the primary word *I-Thou* to him, he is not a thing among things, and does not consist of things."[52] Buber believed that every human being is beyond knowledge, that is, is a bearer of a truth which is unique to that person and is never commanded by the outside observer, not the psychologist, not the doctor or the counselor. At this point, Buber reflects some of the influence of Kierkegaard, who felt that inwardness, our unique knowledge about ourselves, is essential to our being selves. Only the self can speak the truth about the self. Thus to enter an I-Thou relationship one must be willing and ready to have the other person speak the truth about himself or herself just as one speaks for one's own self. No one can force another or manipulate another into an I-Thou encounter. It cannot be staged. It can only happen in a free giving and receiving relationship in which each person in the relationship shares fully and mutually. Buber expressed it in the following manner:

> The primary word *I-Thou* can be spoken only with the whole being. Concentration and fusion into the whole being can never take place through my agency, nor can it ever take place without me. I become through my relation to the *Thou;* as I become *I,* I say *Thou.* All real living is meeting.[53]

Buber did not believe that life could be lived entirely within the I-Thou relationship. It is always and only a happening, a moment, and it ends. Life falls back into the I-It. But it is in the "timeless" present of the I-Thou relationship that we know our separate selves, and encounter the shared presence of another self. Buber writes:

> The world of *It* is set in the context of space and time. The world of *Thou* is not set in the context of either of these. The particular *Thou,* after the relational event has run its course, *is bound* to become an *It.* The particular *It,* by entering the relational event, *may* become a *Thou.*[54]

All of this, for Buber, is set within the context of a biblical theism. There is an Eternal Thou who encounters the human self and, in the encounter, affirms each one in his or her individuality. God, for Buber, is not an invitation to the self's oblivion, but rather the occasion of the self's most radical affirmation—leading on to the world's affirmation as well. God is the one *"Thou"* that does not become an *"It,"*[55] the One also of whom we have intimation in every I-Thou encounter. God is the One who gives final meaning to our encounters and reminds us always of the "other" as person.

Buber's theism is an essential part of what he offers as a statement of the meaning of life, but in relation to the question of technology it is important to underline Buber's central point that authentic personal relations are beyond the technical sphere. Technology is not simply open-ended and experimental; it is most basically the effort to control nature and other human beings. It is advertising, computer-profiling; it is propaganda; it is coercion. In the productive process it demands the conformity of the human to the machine. The propensity of technology is to transform human beings into means, whereas Buber, like the philosopher Immanuel Kant before him, argues that human beings are to be treated "always as ends in themselves, and never as means only."[56] Buber, however, goes beyond Kant in describing the positive nature of human mutuality, the personal exchange between equals, each of whom is free to give *and* receive. All of this defines a realm of personal existence which is sacrificed to technology only at the cost of the human. Thus, technology which operates as though it would know no limit encounters here a limit, a reference point for its criticism.

There is a second point in Buber's *I and Thou* which often escapes notice and is seldom discussed, yet represents also a major point in Buber's appraisal and rejection of the technological imperative. It can be described as the point at which selfhood is most vulnerable to technological subversion. Buber fixes this point—strangely but tellingly—as the human obsession with "experience."

What strikes one as especially strange in Buber's discussion of experience is that for Buber experience is interpreted in essentially negative terms. Our own inclination is to cherish and seek experiences. Buber, however, denies that the I-Thou relation is an experience. It is an event, a happening not fixed in space and time, which only falls back into space and time when it is ended. Buber believed that to enter a relationship in order to "have an experience" was only to deny its possibility. It is to want to "have" something out of a relationship and then, later, to preside over it as a memory, a thing. If experience gathering is the be-all and end-all of human existence then "the other" is inevitably transformed into a means, a means to an experience.

Buber writes:

> Man travels over the surface of things and experiences them. He extracts knowledge about their constitution from them: he wins an experience from them. He experiences what belongs to the things. But the world is not presented to man by experiences alone. These present him only with a world composed of *It* and *He* and *She* and *It* again. . . . The man who experiences has not part in the world. For it is "in him" and not between him and the world that the experience arises.[57]

This argument may be hard for the contemporary reader to assimilate. The tendency is to read and to puzzle a little—and to pass on; for most of us are probably convinced, or simply take for granted, that the "chief purpose of life, of everyone's life, is to collect experiences." This is "enjoyment" or "enrichment": the continuous collection of experiences over the course of a lifetime. Buber says no to this because it rules out the possibility of personal encounters in which each person risks his or her whole being in trust and mutuality. Of course, encounters may occur which move beyond the original intention of "experiencing," but Buber suggests that we are essentially dealing here with a deficient understanding of selfhood. The human self is *not*, for Buber, a center *of* and *for* experience, an empty vessel to be filled with experience. The self for Buber is a *person*, an identifiable "who," a who of value in-and-of itself.

Buber does not describe how we in the modern day have come to focus so much on experience as the definitive form of meaning. He simply rejects it. But here it can be suggested that in our passage from the sixteenth century to the eighteenth and on to the twentieth the human community has lost successively first heaven (the past religious focus of meaning), then the future (the political hope), and now we have left only experience. Again we return to the point made in chapter 3 above in criticism of Becker, that the Enlightenment substitution of posterity for heaven as the focus of meaning was no simple substitution, that the elimination of heaven as the goal of life introduced disillusion as a major new historical force. To be asked to sacrifice for a future that does not come leads eventually to the abandonment of hope in that future. In lieu of a corporate and future project, we have, each of us, become our own project;[58] and in place of political vision and commitment, we allow technology to bring us its gifts, bring us its flood of possibilities for experience.

Marshall McLuhan suggested that the once new medium of television had extended our senses, enlarged our vision, and presented us with a global village. That certainly is a possible interpretation of the impact of the television medium, but it is also possible to view this technological advance simply as a means of increasing the quantity of our experiences. Daniel Boorstin certainly goes a long way toward defining the essence of technology in such terms. He writes: "The Swiss writer Max Frisch once described technology as 'the knack of so arranging the world that we don't have to experience it.' But in American history technology could equally well be described as 'the knack of so arranging the world as to produce new experiences.' "[59] Again, Boorstin observes:

> The challenge of the Machine was as open-ended as the human spirit. Americans in the latter part of the twentieth century, in defiance of some fashionable woesayers, had more chance than ever before to do the unprecedented. Their problem was not the lack of opportunity for adventure but the shallowness of their human satisfaction and human fulfillment. The American challenge was how to keep alive the sense of quest which had brought the nation into being. How to discover the endless novelties of the Machine. . . . How to do a thousand still-unimagined works of machine magic without becoming the servant of the Machine or allowing the sense of novelty to pall or the quest for the new to lose its charm.[60]

Boorstin has in fact here described precisely how we have become the servants of the Machine. Our political disillusion—and our boredom—haunt us and we look to technology precisely for novelty and new experience. By contrast it would be Buber's view that with our technological "progress" we have actually settled for a lesser statement of the human.[61] D'Alembert and Condorcet would, I think, agree. Jefferson and Melville and Lincoln too.[62]

In the next chapter we will turn to a discussion of the theological response—or lack thereof—to the technological challenge. The question to be asked is How have those who once took heaven so seriously answered the call to address the world—this technological world? We do so by first addressing a recently defined problem in the relation of theology to technology and then by offering assessment of two major twentieth-century theologies, questioning their adequacy in dealing with the technological issue.

5
TECHNOLOGY AND THEOLOGY

The historian Lynn White, Jr., in his 1963 article "What Accelerated Technological Progress in the Western Middle Ages?,"[1] entertained the thought that a unique and positive relation existed between the religious tradition and the distinctive growth of technology in medieval Europe. While noting two secular factors at work in the growth of Western technology, to wit, native Celtic craftsmanship and a peculiar receptiveness to innovation resulting from the barbaric invasions, White devoted his major attention to an assessment of the role of religion in the accelerated development of European technology. Here he attempted to delineate between an Eastern Christian spiritual ethos and a Western one. Since both traditions, along with Judaism, share a common rejection of primitive animism and thus affirmed the "disenchantment" of nature, White suggested the need to identify an additional key factor in the rapid technological advance of the West. This, he suggested, was a voluntaristic, work-oriented spirituality common to Western monasticism and standing in contrast to the more contemplative spirituality of Eastern Orthodoxy. In Western monasteries physical labor was integrated with spiritual discipline, a phenomenon expressed in the maxim: "To work is to pray." White argued that the linkage of disciplined intellectual endeavor with physical labor led to a pervasive democratic spirit in Western monasteries and a concern to alleviate those kinds of work "unworthy of a child of God."[2] Thus there developed on the soil of Western spirituality the effort "to substitute a power machine for a man" wherever human labor bore the character of bestial labor. Monastic communities, White suggested, became centers of technological change, disseminating various kinds of laborsaving technology from the course of the twelfth century on.

In 1967, however, White underwent a significant change in attitude toward the whole technological enterprise. Growing concern with the ecological crisis led White to de-emphasize the humane, democratic, laborsaving theme expressed earlier and to accent instead Western society's exploitative and abusive attitude toward nature. In this later article, entitled "The Historical Roots of Our Ecological Crisis,"[3] White charged that Christianity (and Judaism) by denying a divine, or semidivine status to nature, by abandoning the animistic reverence for the forces of nature, paved the way for the modern technological drive to subdue the natural order and exploit it for human purposes.

The generality of much of White's 1967 argument is somewhat surprising as one rereads it after twenty-plus years. He makes major use of a widely argued theological point of the late nineteenth and the early twentieth century, one that J. B. Bury and others had cited in attempting to account for the rise of the concept of Progress[4]—the idea that biblical religion is basically oriented toward history rather than nature as the bearer of revelation. White used much of the same historical data found in his earlier 1963 article, but in place of the emphasis upon the emerging medieval, "democratic" commitment to a more humane workplace, White now stressed the exploitative character of the Western development of the heavy plow, the rapid spread of water and windmills. White's account of the biblical basis for all this centered on the verse in Genesis 1:28 in which God enjoined the newly created man and woman to "be fruitful and multiply, and fill the earth and subdue it; and have dominion over the fish of the sea and over every living thing that moves upon the earth."[5] In offering comment on the biblical disenchantment of nature, White observed, "By destroying pagan animism Christianity made it possible to exploit nature in a mood of indifference to the feelings of natural objects." And he concluded, "Hence we shall continue to have a worsening ecologic crisis until we reject the Christian axiom that nature has no reason for existence save to serve man."[6]

This 1967 article by White captured well the spirit of the counterculture and the burgeoning ecological movement of the late 1960s and early 1970s, but it also elicited a widespread critical response from the theological community. Many theologians took issue with White's characterization of the dominant Christian attitude toward nature as one of "exploitation," countering with the claim that the much longer and more widely based biblical teaching is one of "stewardship." Also the long-standing theological tradition of natural law, especially strong during the Middle Ages, hardly supports White's general thesis, since natural law maintained that a divinely ordained order of nature established binding guidelines for human behavior, a view still argued today in Roman Catholic circles, for example, on the question of birth control.[7] Nature, in this important tradition, served as bearer of God's command and could hardly be seen as the object of human exploitation or indifference.

In a 1975 review and assessment of White's argument, Thomas S. Derr gave account of the historical background for White's argument, summed up subsequent criticism, and then offered his own statement of ethical dissent. Derr sharply challenged White's departure from his earlier-held views on the humane, laborsaving nature of technological developments in the West and questioned White's efforts to "re-enchant" the order of nature on the pattern of St. Francis of Assisi. In commenting on White's new theme of ecological angst, Derr asked if White was perhaps on the brink of some new form of "paganism, authoritarianism, and brutality"[8] suggested also by Garrett Hardin's notorious "lifeboat ethics" of the early 1970s.[9]

Derr's comments are very much to the point. Some of his ethical concerns parallel those of Lewis Mumford, who argued, years earlier, that "nature" can generate its own peculiar "technological" abuse. As described above, Mumford suggested that ancient Egypt was marked by a remarkable "technological exhibitionism" established on the order of nature and centered on the sun as divine. Mumford commented:

> The organizers of [Egyptian society] derived their power and authority from a heavenly source. Cosmic order was the basis of this new human order. The exactitude in measurement, the abstract mechanical system, the compulsive regularity of this "megamachine" . . . sprang directly from astronomical observations and scientific calculations. This inflexible, predictable order, incorporated later in the calendar, was transferred to the regimentation of the human components.[10]

Mumford wrote that the great symbol of this age, the pyramid, "was effected with only small, modest, mechanically primitive instruments: chisels, saws, mallets, ropes. The huge stones that were transported for miles to the pyramids at Giza were borne on wooden sledges, and raised into position without the aid of a wheel, a pulley, a windlass, or a derrick, or even any animal power except that of mechanized men."[11] Mumford makes the point that nature could give rise to models of extreme human oppression and degradation, and this is the burden also of Derr's concern.

In his criticism of White, Derr steers shy of questioning White's historical analysis, limiting himself chiefly to a critique of White's "Christian compassion." Derr warns:

> In finally taking his stand where he does, White may be paying a fearful price. The danger is not from critics of his historical judgments; history is his business and he can handle attacks from that quarter. The problem is

that the values he has espoused throughout his career—Christian, democratic, humane—are likely to be subverted by people making even perfectly legitimate use of "Historical Roots."[12]

Here, however, Derr's stance of "history is his business" is inadequate. How White reads history and his prescription for a cure is very much at issue. As a medievalist devoted to the study of technology White has made a major contribution to broadening our understanding of technology and the development of machines during the so-called Dark Ages. But a flaw in White's historical argument must also be noted: White falls victim to what is termed the "genetic fallacy," the supposition that by describing the "origins" of a phenomenon one has somehow given account of what that phenomenon subsequently is or has become in the course of history. White is very guarded in his use of the term "cause" in describing the acceleration of technological progress during the Middle Ages. He writes: "No historian in our time dares use the word *cause*. Historical understanding is arrived at, these days, less in terms of causes, in the vernacular sense, than through the isolation of various elements in an historical situation which seem to exert a 'gravitational' influence upon each other and to move in a cluster in the direction of the movement which we are trying to comprehend."[13]

Yet despite these earlier scholarly qualifications, the subsequent burden of White's analysis in "Historical Roots" is to identify an orthodox Christian attitude toward nature and propose it as the chief cause of our present ecological crisis. He charges that "Christianity bears a huge burden of guilt"[14] for the crisis. Not only is Genesis 1:28 at fault (and thus Judaism as well) but also that peculiar "voluntaristic" or activistic spirituality of Western Christianity. Since both science *and* technology are outgrowths of the biblical disenchantment of nature, White asserts that the solution for the ecological crisis cannot lie with science and technology alone. White declares, "Both our present science and our present technology are so tinctured with orthodox Christian arrogance toward nature that no solution for our ecologic crisis can be expected from them alone. Since the roots of our trouble are so largely religious the remedy must also be essentially religious whether we call it that or not."[15] Thus White offers his own prescription for a recultivation of Franciscan animism or panpsychism.

If one recalls recent theological history, the early and mid-1960s were marked by a preoccupation with secular theology. During this period, a generation of younger, post–World War II theologians sought to leave behind the heavier tones of continental theology (Barth, Bultmann, and others) and picked up on some themes found in Dietrich Bonhoeffer's *Letters and Papers from Prison*. They sought to translate Christian life and thought into the secular idiom. The most popular rendering of secular theology was Harvey Cox's *The Secular City*. In this book Cox argued that since biblical religion gave rise to the "disenchantment of nature," the "desacralization of politics," and the "deconsecration of values,"[16] the Christian should view the secular order essentially in positive rather than negative terms. Cox argued that the Christian should seek to integrate faith into the secular order.

What is common to both the outlooks of secular theology and White's "Historical Roots" is the assumption of a biblical, theological basis for the secular order (inclusive of science and technology); but what is different in White from Cox is the judgment that secular dynamics (expansiveness, mobility, urban culture) represent threat (ecological crisis) rather than liberating promise. At issue here are differing appraisals of technology. What both White and secular theology tended to neglect in the analysis of "roots" were the critical historical developments which have taken place *since* the Middle Ages and which created the concrete reality of the secular option. The history that comes to bear at this point is the devastating fratricidal religious wars of the sixteenth and seventeenth centuries, the liberating psychological impact of the Copernican-Newtonian revolution, a positive experience of social and political change, the emergence of new hopes, and finally the increasing affirmation of this-worldly goals and purposes in contrast to past otherworldliness. Against the view of White, if Genesis 1:28 has come to bear special meaning in the course of history, it has taken on much of that meaning in the context of these later events and not as the condition for them. In addition, with these same critical events and the concomitant revision of historical meaning (the rise in the belief in Progress) came the troubling onset of disillusion, the disturbing awareness of unfulfilled hopes following in the train of historical struggle and sacrifice. Then came also the worldly "balm" of industrialization and material abundance, the consolation and the lure (power, adventure) of technology.

In this context, disillusion in the form of ecological crisis is less apparent and initially less acute than that associated with political history. Here the ambiguity of technology as both cause and cure moderates anxiety and lessens despair. Christianity after this time, after "Enlightenment"—and even after the second "enlightenment" (disillusion)—cannot hope to reintegrate Western culture on theological grounds, or on the basis of a new, baptized metaphysics ("Process" thought). Rather, it must be seen that technology, on secular grounds, has come to serve as the self-healing "physician," a lesser good than the political-social hope (e.g., the classless society, a "more perfect union")—and also as a *distraction,* even though, ecologically speaking, it may finally be a fatal distraction.

Theology, however, has still not come to terms with this history,[17] with technology as the context of and challenge to faith. Thus we turn to consider briefly two theologies that point up the inadequacy. One is a theology of cultural integration (Tillich); the other, a theology of political hope (Moltmann). Positively, what can be said of both theologies is that they have addressed the malaise of historical disillusion, but then, as we have argued, so also has technology.

To attempt to summarize the theology of Paul Tillich (1886–1965) is no small task, since his thought is at points convoluted and obscure. Such an effort is called for because Tillich stands as a classic system builder, one who offers to put everything in place, promising the inquirer an aesthetic sense of wholeness.

Among the many aims of Tillich's theology was the effort to recast Christian thought and Christian self-awareness in such a way as to recapture an encompassing sense of meaning. Tillich is a very important figure among many who are haunted by the past grandeur of a Christian culture and who are dissatisfied with the lessened role of Christian faith within the framework of modernity. Tillich's intent, in his system, was to escape the religious ghetto and universalize once more the scope and nature of faith.

As mentioned in chapter 2 above, in *The Courage to Be,* Tillich identified three embracing human problems which, at different times, have commanded the focus of Christian concern.[18] In the earliest period, in Roman times, Christianity sought to answer the question of death; in the Middle Ages the central question was guilt; and in the modern period prime concern has centered on the problem of meaninglessness. Tillich in his theology sought primarily to address this latter question, asserting simultaneously its universality in the modern era and its answer in faith.

In arguing the answer of faith, Tillich insisted that the traditional concept of God had to be set aside. He offered two reasons for this. In the first place, Tillich believed that Christian isolation within the modern world stemmed in large measure from the conception of God as person, God as transcendent "other." Tillich never tired of asserting, against traditional theism, that God as "a being" is only a part of a larger whole, that to conceive of God as *a* being is to affirm a reality greater than God, to wit, "Being-Itself." Being-itself, Tillich insisted, lies beyond the subject-object dichotomy, beyond all separation and isolation.[19] Religion, he declared, "is the state of being grasped by the power of being itself. . . . [It] is never completely absent. For everything that is participates in being-itself, and everybody has some awareness of this participation." Faith, Tillich argued, "is the state of being grasped by the power of being which transcends everything that is and in which everything that is participates."[20] With this concept of God—and faith—Tillich rejected, on first principle, all parochial religion. Atheism also was ruled out, since everyone who affirmed his or her own being in some measure believed and participated in the reality of God ("Being-Itself").

The second reason Tillich gave for doing away with traditional theism was that such a belief gives rise to the sense of God as "tyrant," as threat to the self. By contrast, Tillich affirmed from his early days the principle of autonomy, the principle that there is no truth which is not simultaneously a truth of the self. In an autobiographical account Tillich noted that his own personal achievement of independence and maturity came about in the course of philosophical debate with his strict, Lutheran father. Tillich remarked on this experience: "It [was] . . . this difficult and painful breakthrough to autonomy which has made me immune against any system of thought or life which demands the surrender of this autonomy."[21] The application of this principle in Tillich's thought led to his rejection of all doctrinal orthodoxies and to his embrace of "symbol" as the proper medium for the communication of religious truth. Meanings, he held, are conveyed through symbols in a nonauthoritative manner: one is "grasped" by the truth of a symbol, one "senses" truth rather than subscribing to a proposition. The truth about Being-Itself is of such a nature. At some fundamental level all people share in the truth about God. Doubt about traditional creeds should be understood as a positive thing, since to doubt is to affirm at a deeper level belief in the Truth. In line with this proposal, Tillich argued early on that just as the doctrine of justification by faith ruled out the doing of good deeds as a means of achieving salvation, so also it ruled out the doing of a "good work of the mind," a belief in the unbelievable, as a means to the same end.[22] To affirm God as *a* being, Tillich believed, was to hark back to an earlier age with all its heteronomous, authoritarian modes of perception and practice, something completely alien to the modern day.[23]

What Tillich offered in this philosophical-theological construction was a *dynamic* view of God (Being-Itself), a concept standing in contrast to the static medieval idea of God as "Perfect Being" or "the Absolute." In place of the medieval concept of reason as the bond between the human and the divine (the basis for the medieval cultural synthesis), Tillich proposed *creativity* as the point of identity between humanity and God.[24] As all persons affirm their own existence so they affirm a reason for being, an "ultimate concern" (synonymous with faith), and seek to realize or actualize purpose or meaning. Just as God stands beyond the subject-object cleavage so human beings transcend, if only momentarily, that same cleavage in their creative activities. Through human creative endeavor, objects, and social-political structures as well, are transformed into bearers of new, more fulfilling meanings.[25] Thus Tillich spoke, in 1919 and throughout the 1920s, of a "theology of culture"; and he defined the effort to bring into being a new, fulfilling cultural era as the great task and challenge of post–World War I Europe.

All of this was embodied in Tillich's concept of the *kairos* (a critical turning point in history), which dominated his thought through World War II. But even after World War II, when his "kairos" idea (a social-historical phenomenon) was de-emphasized in favor of the concept of "New Being" (a category more open to individualistic interpretation),[26] Tillich maintained the fundamental nature of creative endeavor. Not only the philosophers, the poets, the statesmen, but common people as well, were involved in the creative process. Tillich writes:

> Spiritual self-affirmation occurs in every moment in which man lives creatively in the various spheres of meaning. Creative, in this context, has the sense not of original creativity as performed by the genius but of living spontaneously in action and reaction with the contents of one's cultural life. . . . Everyone who lives creatively in meanings affirms himself as a participant in these meanings. He affirms himself as receiving and transforming reality creatively.[27]

In another work Tillich says: "A person who participates in a culture's movement, growth, and possible destruction is culturally creative. In this sense, every human being is culturally creative, simply by virtue of speaking and using tools."[28]

It should be apparent from this brief summary of Tillich's system that there is small room here for a quarrel with technology. For the larger part of his philosophical-theological career Tillich was chiefly concerned to address the social-political crisis of Europe following World War I. He hoped and worked for a European cultural rebirth. His kairos concept envisioned simultaneously the passing of an old order and the birth of a new one in which the fragmentary nature of social and political life would find a healing wholeness in a "religious-socialist" cultural renewal.[29] The kairos idea was designed to avoid the disillusion of Marxist utopianism in favor of a more modest, temporally limited, political and cultural rebirth, one which Tillich argued would give place in its turn to a future "judgment" and "new creation." Writing to a former colleague in 1934, Tillich recalled the occasion of the formulation of the kairos idea.

We did not want to destroy the burden of the demand and the passion of the expectation. In this need—I can remember exactly the day—the kairos idea was discovered. It was discovered—as perhaps many do not know—in the struggle with the problem of utopia. Hereby a position was provided from which we had the possibility of appreciating the significance of the historical moment for the structuring of the future without becoming utopians.[30]

However, even Tillich's nonutopian kairos concept fell victim to disillusion. In Germany it was overwhelmed by the greater passion of National Socialism. In fact, the generality, the vagueness, of Tillich's conceptualization allowed the use of many of his ideas, the kairos concept itself, in the Nazi cause—this after Tillich left Germany in 1933.[31] Thus it was that after World War II, in the later 1940s, the kairos idea yielded to a new individualistic emphasis, drawing upon psychoanalytic themes which Tillich had previously shunned.[32]

In his earlier affirmation of the kairos idea, Tillich was of course committed to social-political expectations and largely ignored technology as a problem;[33] but, later with the turn to individualistic motifs, with the new emphasis upon psychoanalytic insight, Tillich came to view the "technical society" as a special problem. In a 1953 discussion, he argued that the growth of the technical, industrial society during the nineteenth and twentieth centuries triggered the existentialist protest. Tillich wrote: "It is my understanding of the movement which is called Existentialism and which is at least one hundred years old that it rebels in the name of personality against the depersonalizing forces of technical society."[34] Our own historical account, by contrast, suggests that existentialism rose to prominence with the collapse of meaning associated with the social, political belief in Progress and was related only in a secondary fashion to technology as such. In fact the shifting pattern in Tillich's own thought, the movement from social-political kairos to the individualistic conception of the "New Being" mirrors well the dynamic of disillusion, moving from corporate to individualistic modes of meaning.[35]

This shift in perspective alters the assessment of technology and of the technical society. The human social involvement is painted in different hues. Along with all the competition for power and the lure of the new, come also the solace of distraction and a subtle revision in the human self-image. The technical society, I suggest, must be viewed in some measure as a consolation, a movement forward to something lesser, "beyond freedom and dignity."[36] It represents, in its strange way, an argument of progress against Progress.

Tillich, to be sure, is able to express all the common concerns about the technical society, the threat of dehumanization, the dominance of means over ends, the possible stifling of creativity within the culture at large.[37] Of a technology-dominated society Tillich says:

> More people have more occasion to encounter the cultural contents of past and present than in any pre-industrial civilization. But it also means that these contents become cultural "goods," sold and bought after they have been deprived of the ultimate concern they represented when originally created. They cease to be a matter of "to be or not to be" for the person. They become matters of entertainment, sensation, sentimentality, learning, weapons of competition, or social prestige, and lose in this way the power of mediating a spiritual center to the person.[38]

Despite such important insight, Tillich is unable to offer a clear statement of an alternative to be affirmed in response to the drift into technological preoccupations. He speaks—because "the system" dictates such speech—of resistance to the technical society in the form of "partial nonparticipation"; but opposition can be only *partial* because all things, all creation, all toolmaking, participate in Being-Itself. Tillich affirms the necessity of accenting personhood in the face of dehumanizing tendencies in technical society, but he makes clear that the source of opposition, of partial nonparticipation, is the "New Reality" which "transcends Christianity as well as non-Christianity, which is anticipated everywhere in history."[39] "Together with the philosophers of life, the Existentialists, the depth psychologists, . . . [Christians] must show how 'the structure of objectivation' (transforming life and person partly into a thing, partly into a calculating machine) permeates all realms of life."[40]

Tillich, while emphasizing "person" in the form of creative individuality, has very little to say about community. His call to Christian action suggests that the noncommunal agents of vitality, the philosophers of life (Friedrich Nietzsche and others) and the existentialists, are equivalent to those who find the meaning of "person" spelled out primarily in a community of acceptance and positive personal interchange. As ever "the human," defined in terms of "autonomy" and exemplified in the artist-creator, stands at the center of Tillich's conceptual world. He writes: "In alliance with all these movements Christian action must attack wherever social patterns become visible by which persons are treated as means or transferred [transformed?] into things, or *deprived of their freedom to decide and to create*."[41] But this really is not enough! It is not person as creative agent who is threatened by the technical society; it is person, active and sustained in a caring community, who is at risk in the individualistic "republic of technology."

In point of fact, it must be said that Tillich's perception of technology fails to note how creative the technological enterprise actually is, and how closely it parallels, as a phenomenon, the main lines of his system. It clearly embodies the principle of autonomy and shuns heteronomy: no technical achievement is regarded as final; the process of technological creation is open-ended, constantly moving on to new creation—and this very much parallels the substance of Tillich's Christology. It can be imagined that every technical breakthrough, every technical "solution" bears for the individual involved—and for the appreciative critic—an "ecstasy" and "exhilaration" not unlike Tillich's own moment of ecstasy as he stood before Botticelli's *Madonna with Singing Angels* in a museum in Berlin in 1918.[42] Cannot the observer stand equally in awe of the medieval invention of the escapement mechanism in the weight-driven clock, or the high vaulting in medieval cathedrals, or the marvel of the iron horse, or the majestic first iron railroad bridges? Tillich certainly would—must—affirm such creativity, but he would perhaps scale down their significance vis-à-vis the works of "high culture," suggesting that they lacked sufficient "depth." But, just as Tillich's system was applied to other than his intended purposes in the past,[43] so can it easily and confidently be claimed by those devoted to the technological enterprise. Creativity is creativity; autonomy, autonomy.

In a later discussion of the question of technology, coming from his last years,[44] Tillich suggested a somewhat more deep-rooted conflict between a "horizontal," temporal pattern of meaning dominated by technological advance and a "vertical," mystical dimension of meaning. In this latter form of meaning, life strives "toward what transcends the cosmos, namely the transcendent One, the ultimate in being and meaning." In his last lecture, Tillich described space exploration as "the greatest triumph of the horizontal line over the vertical," but maintained that a rebirth of vertical meaning was still to come. Tillich asserted that "human nature is not expressed in its full potentialities by the horizontal line. Sooner or later it will revolt against the latter's predominance."[45]

Here one recognizes the persistence of the kairos hope which had earlier dominated Tillich's thought, the longing for an autonomous historical development filled with the sense of "unconditional" meaning (the sense either of "depth," or of "transcendence"). In the end one is struck with the great difficulty of sorting out the inchoate meanings that are suggested by Tillich's essentially aesthetic-romantic view of life. Also, one is left with the alternative of either trying to give his system meaning within the framework of technical society or waiting wistfully for some new outpouring of meaning that may come in the future. One has finally to ask whether his efforts at a synthesis of culture and religion command credibility in the face of the actuality of a world of VCRs, computers, and genetic engineering; whether they represent an adequate interpretation of Christian content. Finally, in advising "nonparticipation" in technology, even though qualified as "partial," Tillich undermined the logic of his entire system. The "theology of culture" becomes "myth" in the common meaning of that term.

If Tillich's theology was set forth amid what Tillich viewed as the "creative chaos" left in the wake of World War I, the theology of Jürgen Moltmann (1926–) took shape against the background of World War II, the Nazi holocaust, the guilt of Germany. It was inevitable that a German theologian, after the war, would address the problem not only of shattered historical expectations but the reasons for the German political-social failure represented by National Socialism. A major reason for this failure, Moltmann felt, was to be found in the Lutheran tradition of submissiveness to political authority. Speaking favorably of the Calvinist tradition in this connection, Moltmann observed:

> To be obedient to God in the political order means to participate directly or indirectly in the practice of political rule. The active resistance for the sake of the oppressed neighbor is not only a right but also a duty of the Christian. The way in which Calvinism bases the state and its constitution theologically on the covenant with God and gives moral sanction to the duty of resistance against the violation of that constitution is more pertinent than ever to the contemporary political dilemma which Christians face. German history could have developed differently if the churches in Germany had adopted this political ethic and had not cultivated the disposition to be submissive to authority.[46]

Moltmann's concern was chiefly centered on the future—in part, it can be suggested, as a means of atoning for the past, an effort also to overcome profound disillusion. In affirming the future Moltmann faced the challenge of claiming purpose for renewed political struggle. In the German context, the moral despair, added to the postwar frustration of the Cold War, was not conducive to the framing of a hopeful political program. Moltmann, however, took up the challenge and framed a political theology centered on the concept of hope. "If it is hope," writes Moltmann, "that maintains and upholds faith and keeps it moving on, if it is hope that draws the believer into the life of love, then it will also be hope that is the mobilizing and driving force of faith's thinking, of its knowledge of, and reflections on, human nature, history and society." With this affirmation of hope Moltmann argued that the ultimate nature of Christian hope, looking forward to "a new creation of all things by the God of the resurrection of Jesus Christ,"[47] allows the hope of faith to catch up, renew, stimulate, and relativize the hopes of the secular order and give them new direction and new inspiration.

> It [Christian hope] will thus outstrip these future visions of a better, more humane, more peaceable world—because of its own "better" promises (Heb. 8.6), because it knows that nothing can be "very good" until "all things are become new." . . . If Christian hope destroys the presumptions in futuristic movements then it does so not for its own sake, but in order to destroy in these hopes the "seeds of resignation," which emerge at the latest with the ideological reign of terror in the utopia in which the hoped for reconciliation with existence becomes an enforced reconciliation.[48]

Just as Tillich, much earlier, had sought to address the problem of disillusion and despair by rejecting utopianism so Jürgen Moltmann has sought to avoid the "seeds of resignation" by proclaiming a different hope which, by the nature of its ultimacy, deprives secular hopes of their "utopian fixity" and transforms them into "provisional, penultimate, and hence flexible goals."[49] This relativizing function of Christian hope, Moltmann maintains, can allow a more positive and realistic embrace of social-political possibilities that in the past have fallen prey to the onslaught of disillusion.

In spelling out his "theology of hope," Moltmann has pursued a much more biblical, theological methodology than did Tillich with his strong philosophical, aesthetic bias. But this does not mean that Moltmann shunned help from "the outside." Although it is possible to trace a variety of roots for his theology of hope,[50] a crucial influential role must be accorded the thought of the neo-Marxist philosopher Ernst Bloch. To be sure, Moltmann makes explicit the major points of divergence between himself and Bloch,[51] but he is clearly dependent upon Bloch for his own formulation of the "future of God" which catches up the past and the present in new forms of meaning. Bloch, the Marxist in search of a nonutopian understanding of history, spoke of the future in terms of "openness," as the occasion/possibility always of a new beginning. Moltmann sums up Bloch's argument in the following account.

> The novel contribution of Ernst Bloch's philosophy is that he does not reduce this openness of man and his hope to mere inwardness, postponing, as it were, his fulfillment to a hereafter. Instead he aligns "man's openness to the world" with an ontology of the world's openness to man. The openness of man which is apparent in his hopes corresponds to the openness of the world process which is apparent in its possibilities. "Reality in process." Everything real goes beyond its processual front into the possible. . . . Only if the category of possibility . . . receives adequate attention can that process be understood in which human hope is mediated with matter so that . . . the "new" of the future can be grasped on the front line of the present.[52]

Moltmann quotes directly from Bloch: " 'That hope, which at any final point, is not satisfied to have reached only its starting point, overcomes the mere cyclic movement.' " And Moltmann then adds his own summary: "Its end point is a new point: its beginning finds meaning only in the end."[53]

"Its beginning finds meaning only in its end;" this stands as a fundamental tenet not only of Bloch's thought, but it bears similarities with the process philosophy of Alfred North Whitehead as well.[54] However, Moltmann is critical of the depersonalized ground for all of this in Bloch's argument. He complains:

> The divine creative impulse is now seen in the core of matter itself. The ever fruitful womb of matter brings forth the forms of being in continually new and rich abundance, and man is the highest realization of its fecundity. The forms and tendencies of history are born from a dialectical mediation of human hopes and the possibilities inherent in nature, of the core of man which is not yet processed out and of the still hidden subject of nature. . . . The transcendence of the creator is made immanent in the creating matter. The demythologization is seen as necessary to the activation of hope. In reality the result is a remythologization of nature. . . . One must ask whether it is necessary to pay such a price for the activation of hope in the process of history.[55]

Moltmann, for himself, holds to a belief in God as personal being. Like Bloch, Moltmann is concerned to revive and sustain human hope. He affirms the proposition: "Its beginning finds meaning only in its end," but the context for this affirmation—and its vital occasion—is the reality of a personal God and the resurrection of Jesus Christ through whom the future takes on creative, new meaning. The future, for Moltmann, becomes a "mode of God's being": God comes to humankind from "tomorrow" rather than from "above." In the resurrection humanity is given a foretaste of the "coming God" through whom all things will be created anew. Jesus, in the resurrection, is translated not into "heaven above" but into the future. Moltmann writes, "The God of the Exodus and the resurrection is the God of the coming kingdom, and therefore a God with future as mode of his being."[56] "God is not the ground of this world and not the ground of existence, but the God of the coming kingdom, which transforms this world and our existence radically. . . . God's being is coming, that is, God is already present in the way in which his future masters the present because his future decides what becomes of the present."[57]

For Moltmann, since the hope of "all things new" relativizes, yet sustains, all earthly hopes—or since all earthly hopes bear the germ of the ultimate hope[58]—Christians must join in the ongoing historical work of creating a new and more just social-political order. Moltmann declares: "To this present world Christian proclamation must give an answer concerning its hope in the future of the crucified one (I Peter 3.15) by conveying to the godless justification and hope of resurrection. We cannot turn our backs on the open horizons of modern history. . . . We must take these horizons up into the eschatological horizon of the resurrection and thereby disclose to modern history its true historic character."[59] He concludes *The Theology of Hope* with the words: "The glory of self-realization and the misery of self-estrangement alike arise from hopelessness in a world of lost horizons. To disclose to it the horizon of the future of the crucified Christ is the task of the Christian Church."[60]

Immersed in the disillusion, guilt, the political catastrophe of twentieth-century Europe, Moltmann offers a brave statement of hope and political responsibility. He is bold in his assertion of long-standing Christian, biblical themes: a personal God, the resurrection of Christ, deliverance, and promise. But one must ask whether Moltmann's, and Bloch's, effort to dispel the specter of despair and energize the *political* will does not also describe what in fact characterizes the technological phenomenon. In speaking of a future that gives new life to the realities of past and present, a future that constantly transforms "ends" into "new beginnings," Moltmann not only diminishes the threat of disillusion but simultaneously poses the problem of "the inexplicable" and "the unintended" as the end result of political struggle and purpose, thereby diminishing that expectation and commitment. To speak thus is also to describe the social-historical dynamics of technology. It can be argued that it is technology, more so than politics, which picks up the unrecognizable in the present and later confronts society with a new reality.

One can illustrate this phenomenon by a reference to what, in journalism, constitutes the newsworthy. In 1951 the *New York Times* celebrated the one-hundredth anniversary of its founding. On that occasion the editors published a volume reproducing what they judged to be the one hundred most newsworthy stories in its history.[61] Almost all the major news stories—as might be expected—had originally appeared as front-page stories dealing with the key events of the Civil War, World War I, the Great Depression, and World War II. Some of the front-page stories dealt with science-technology matters, but of special note is the fact that of the few news items that were treated originally on the back pages of the *Times* and then were accorded major status by the 1951 editors most were technology stories: the invention of the telephone, the electric light, the first flight of the Wright brothers. And one can add to this list also the 1947 announcement of the development of the transistor, a back-page item which the 1951 editors did not see fit to up-grade, but which will likely gain promotion in any future editorial reassessments.

What this interesting project of the 1951 editors of the *New York Times* points up is the power of technology to catch up, in Moltmann's words, our past and present and surprise us with its own future. Moltmann, of course, used this formulation to describe God's coming kingdom, God's future; but one might well substitute the word "technol-ogy" for Moltmann's profferred description of God's future and come up with a valid description of a major historical feature of technology. "God's [read "Technology's"] being is coming, that is, God [technology] is already present in the way in which his [its] future masters the present because his [its] future decides what becomes of the present."[62] It is ironic that Moltmann, in trying to overcome "the misery of self-estrangement" arising "from hopelessness in a world of lost horizons," the shattered world of political expectations, should offer a conceptual remedy (the future as a mode of God's being) which nicely describes the manner in which *technology* also answers the problem of despair. Tech-nology expands the scope of our experience, affords manifold possibili-ties for the satisfaction of human desires, and opens up ever-new opportunities for the pursuit of power. It catches us up in an unex-pected, unplanned future, and this, in the light of the political failure, carries both consolation and appeal.

Standing off from these two contemporary theologies, which seek ear-nestly to answer the perceived problems of the modern human condi-tion—and one could certainly add other theologies to the list,[63] one is forced to ask if they have properly focused on technology as the chief challenge to theology. Not the despair and the meaninglessness which have fallen out from the dissipation of Western society's political expec-tations, not the specter of "the bomb" itself, but the ability of technol-ogy to offer and inculcate another definition of the human:[64] this is the major new challenge to theology.

Supposing this to be so, let us propose that theology—as suggested earlier—must come to terms with its own past and exorcise its medieval theocratic ghost. Have we not all grown weary—within the community of faith—of the tireless "theological" exhortations against atheism, in either the form of homiletic-philosophical scoldings or the subtleties of a "system" which rule it out as a possibility? And should we not also question the theocratic claim implicit in the definitions of "the univer-sal human," for example, creativity in Tillich, hope in Moltmann, or enjoyment in the process theologians? In all these definitions, there is the hidden implication that theology, or ecclesiastical office, whatever its other functions may be, serves also as the patron of culture. Let us suggest instead that technology has brought an end to all this, because historically it now continues its course on fully independent grounds and will seemingly go its way "baptized" or not, chastened or not, serving as its own physician.

The challenge to theology of technology's coming-of-age is for theology to affirm its own proper counterproject of life-in-community. The major task for the believing community is precisely to *be* community, to discover and uncover its own reality as a people of God. Its vocation, as suggested at points in the documents of Vatican II, is to be a "pilgrim church"[65] and a fellowship. And in order to be heard and noted in the technical society, it must speak from an isness and not—as Tillich would have it—from an idealistic "valuating sense of essence" or—with Moltmann—from the perspective of some "final hope." The reality of the church as a communion of believers who share fully in the reciprocities of faith and love is the only counterproject conceivable in the face of the personally fragmenting and community-threatening dynamics of technology's basically rudderless course.

The theological task thus defined may seem small in contrast to the "world-conquering" attraction of system building, but it is not. The task involves a need to examine the Christian community's own commitment to the radical egalitarianism of the gospel, the recognition of the fact that in that gospel a leveling has taken place in which the lowly have been raised up, the mighty humbled. Søren Kierkegaard, of course, was early committed to this actuality.[66] Nietzsche scorned it.[67] There is a question whether Bonhoeffer fully understood it.[68] Feminist theology has certainly helped to define the problem; and liberation theology, in its initiation of base communities, has helped give form to the reality. But theology, let us repeat, cannot be committed to this prospect of the communion of saints and still double-mindedly pretend to some form of medieval theocracy.[69]

One might, by contrast, entertain the notion that theology and the Christian community continually learn from interaction with the secular option, even if now troublingly dominated by technology. In a certain sense the community of faith needs the secular as a corrective to its own religious illusions and presumptions. The secular option serves to help judge the church's moral failures and spiritual arrogance. Certainly it has had a sobering impact upon an exaggerated Christian otherworldliness. One need not abandon the "other world" as some contemporary theologies have done, but certainly the context of faith is fully within *this* world and cannot be centered primarily on the next. Here Bonhoeffer was right in warning Christians against moving too quickly from the this-worldliness of the Old Testament to the otherworldliness of the New.[70] In this connection one must acknowledge an element of truth in Nietzsche's pained complaint that Christianity has waged war "against all that is noble, gay, high-minded on earth, against our happiness on earth."[71] When, in the past, the reality of the other world drained off concern for this one, how did humanity gain? in the Crusades? in the Inquisition? in inhuman fanaticisms?

Yet, to affirm only this world does not assure that one has gained freedom from illusion. This, after all, was a major point in Carl Becker's *Heavenly City of the Eighteenth-Century Philosophers:* the fanaticisms once associated with the "other world" found new expression in this one. The "enlightened," Becker noted, were also filled with "enthusiasm." And even Becker, with his cynicism, bore the seeds of illusion, especially in relation to the promise of technology—his hope that technology would instill a redemptive rationality.[72] In short, if the secular order constitutes a ground of criticism against Christian otherworldliness,[73] so the community of faith serves as a critique of the depersonalizing and spiritually anarchic tendencies within the technological-secular sphere.

In its inception, when the secular order embraced the vision of a perfected humanity and a new human community, important segments of the community of faith could identify with the efforts to achieve such a goal. In that situation a collapse of faith into the general cultural situation was understandable.[74] But with the decline of that vision and its supersession by the rise to dominance of the "technological imperative," it has become more difficult to find in the secular sphere reflections of a substantive Christian purpose. The efforts to construct a secular theology in the late 1960s foundered not only in the storms of student, black, and feminist protest but also on the shoals of the emerging ecological crisis.[75] What the present critique of the secular presupposes is not the ultimacy of the Christian hope, as Moltmann would have it, but simply the persistence of the actualities—and hopes—of a Christian, human belonging. In this context the acknowledgment of sin within the Christian community represents the refusal, on the basis of God's grace, to abandon the political possibility.

This in turn means that along with the theological task of uncovering and discovering Christian community, there emerges a simultaneous commitment to mission. Since Christian faith is in major part the perseverance in a common life in *this* world, it demands the sustenance of that world both in its social-political and environmental aspects. Faith also carries the implicit assumption of a wider redemptive purpose, a healing that goes beyond its own existence. Socially and politically this entails a committed struggle to maintain and enhance the varied means of justice and healing against the encroachments of ever-new configurations of privilege and power, changes made possible by technology's onward surge. Tillich, in one of his keener observations, called attention to "the growth of esoteric groups who through their knowledge and their inventiveness by far surpass what can be reached even by highly learned and productive people, not to speak of the vast majority of human beings. Such elites are esoteric and exclusive, partly through natural selection, partly through public prestige, partly through skillful exercise of their power."[76]

In the face of such extrapolitical concentrations of power, there is need to be reminded of John Calvin's dictum that the purpose of government is to assure "that humanity . . . be maintained among men."[77] Theology is called to nurture awareness of the need to assess critically the rationalizations and assumptions of technological innovation. As participants in the project of community building, both in the church setting and the larger context of society, the people of faith must be prepared to question the course of technology, marking its claims, helping to fix responsibilities, and attempting always to assess its communal impact.

To see the task of theology in these terms is not to define some new role for the discipline—only to deny to it the presumptive role of serving as God's cultural surrogate. Theology is community-bound, faith-bound, history-bound. Technology is perhaps inadvertently calling theology to its proper and worthy task.

6

SUMMATION AND THEOLOGICAL POSTSCRIPT

In this book we have attempted to explicate major aspects of the modern phenomenon of technology, primarily in its changing social and political roles. We have suggested that this is best done by setting it in the context of the Western belief in Progress. We have noted that technology in our time has essentially taken over the meaning of the term "progress," replacing previously deeply held political hopes and expectations. The erosion of political hope in the West has come about not as a result of the rise of technology per se but in conjunction with it. A major factor at cause in this decline of political vision is the phenomenon of disillusion, a much neglected offshoot of the major seventeenth- to eighteenth-century shift from a religious, otherworldly understanding of meaning to a secular, this-worldly form of meaning. By providing material benefits, enlarging the scope of experience, redirecting the sense of adventure, and offering always new opportunities for the pursuit of power, technology has claimed the dominant role in modern Western culture. Its "autonomous," uncontrolled course (Mumford, Ellul, Winner) stems in major part from its diffuse character and its capacity to provide distraction and novelty, needs arising in part from the decline of social-political meaning. Technology addresses and reinforces the fragmenting, individualistic tendencies of modern society. If it has, in our time, redefined the world as a global village, the village it offers is without kinship and enduring social bonds. Ethnic and religious loyalties persist as expressions of social value, but these continue in spite of—and in some cases in reaction to—the technological enterprise. At this point in time, one is forced to ask whether technology, if at one time it served the purpose of human dignity, does not now chiefly cultivate human sensuousness, enhancing every form of sensory pleasure—and of power. On this course, nature has become not so much a threat to be combated as a resource to be consumed.

To be sure, this reading of history and our present condition will appear to some people, probably many, as somewhat cranky, since technology has worn so proudly the mantle of cultural approval. But it can be said on behalf of our proffered reading that it sheds helpful light upon what is transpiring on the present stage of history. We note that in this last decade of the twentieth century the Soviet Union, a major expression of political hope—however dubious that Marxist hope may appear to have been to many—is undergoing a huge spasm of change. This change in the Soviet Union is at root the outworking of that powerful historical force: disillusion.[1] The Soviet experiment in hope is clearly in decline, a decline triggered in part by technology, but especially by political disenchantment. *Glasnost* and *perestroika* under the leadership of Mikhail Gorbachev have come as the culmination of a series of ideological setbacks that earlier undermined the expectation of achieving socialism: the Stalin purges of the 1930s, Titoism[2] after World War II, Nikita Khrushchev's landmark de-Stalinization speech of February 1956, the Soviet break with Red China in 1959 followed by the growth of independent Communist parties throughout Europe in the 1960s and 1970s.[3] With Gorbachev has come the recognition that the Soviet system cannot compete technologically with the West and Japan. This has led to the effort to introduce a larger measure of freedom into the Soviet system—a freedom, however, which was offered originally not as a political concept but as a corrective for technological lag, a pragmatic effort to upgrade Soviet technology and stimulate a lethargic economy. This development has been warmly welcomed on the international scene; it presages an easing of ideological conflict and thus also the danger of military conflict, at least among the major powers.

This development, at the same time, affords further illustration of the decline of the "political idea," the commitment to something beyond ethnic loyalties, to some more inclusive basis of human community. Technology cannot fill this vacuum, for technology does not move toward this end. The freedom it fosters serves only its own well-being. Thus, where a unifying political idea is dissipating—as in the Soviet Union—the question arises: What is to contain the centrifugal forces at work in that political body? What will become of the *Union* of Soviet Socialist Republics? Events have transpired so rapidly on this front that a passage of weeks outdates most expectations. Yet the question continues to haunt.

This is an immediate drama, but not one for secret satisfaction, not at least in the United States. We can well ask whether our own great experiment in political vision, a "more perfect union" beyond the mere "pursuit of happiness,"[4] is not languishing amid our own centrifugal forces:

the growth of class consciousness, the corrosive nature of multinational corporate power, the erosion of the social infrastructure fashioned by previous generations, and the reassertion of ethnic loyalties. Here also questions are being raised about the "habits of the heart," about "individualism and commitment in American life."[5]

Strange. Is it the case that the two great supraethnic political experiments are suffering similar maladies, differing in some respects and in degree of acuteness, but now alike in their surrender to the technological and economic enterprise? Here, however, technology is not able to serve as physician: technology is without a cure for the human longing for meaningful community. In fact, technology represents only a lingering spiritual death, which, on its present course, and in league with the profit motive and human greed, portends physical death as well. Writing not long ago in the *New York Times*, the columnist Flora Lewis argued that though the Cold War was abating "there are many signs that the next general international crisis is going to be about the environment. It can become as abrasive, dangerous and costly as the arms race."[6] And not long afterward, in a nationally published commentary, Dr. George M. Woodwell, director of the Woods Hole Research Center in Massachusetts, voiced a growing international concern:

> There are limits to the thesis that the free market rations resources by adjusting prices, forcing substitutions as resources become dear. Nowhere are these limits more apparent than in the wastes that threaten the common resources of air, land and water, and nowhere are the failures more threatening than in the global changes now underway. . . . Scientists are urgently concerned about changes that become irreversible—the pollution of the oceans with persistent toxins, the destruction of forests by acid rain and other airborne pollutants, the continued and unrelenting destruction of life around the globe. But they are even more concerned that these erosive effects will be amplified by rapid climactic change caused by the release of heat-trapping gases into the atmosphere: the global heat trap. The effects have potential for destructive changes in the human condition as profound as nuclear war. If current patterns of growth are not deflected by plan, they will be stopped haphazardly, even disastrously, by the erosion of the global environment.[7]

Woodwell suggests that technology must be given a focus, a direction, which it does not now manifest, that the survival of humanity in a natural environment looms as the issue of our time.

Let us conclude with a theological postscript and an agenda. All of the above concerns derive from a shared history—one common to the nations of Europe, America, and now the world. Theology, however, is bound to a special history entwined within the common one—the history of faith and grace—a history that a believing community has consistently turned to for present instruction and insight.

I turn to Calvin, a figure frequently scorned by moderns as a moral tyrant, perhaps lacking the genius of Luther,[8] but one who intuitively grasped something of—and contributed distinctively to—an emerging modern world.[9]

In 1539, Calvin penned noteworthy words in response to a letter from Cardinal Jacopo Sadoleto to the City Council of Geneva, enjoining the Genevans to abandon "innovation" and return to the medieval church. In his reply Calvin wrote:

> As to your preface, which, in proclaiming the excellence of eternal blessedness, occupies a third part of your letter, it cannot be necessary for me to dwell long in reply. . . . [It] is not very sound theology to confine a man's thoughts so much to himself, and not to set before him, as the prime motive of existence, zeal to illustrate the glory of God. . . . It certainly is the part of a Christian . . . to ascend higher than merely to seek and secure the salvation of his own soul. I am persuaded, therefore, that there is no man imbued with true piety, who will not consider as insipid that long and labored exhortation to zeal for heavenly life, a zeal which keeps a man entirely devoted to himself, and does not, even by one expression, arouse him to sanctify the name of God.[10]

This remarkable rejection of spiritual narcissism and the medieval fixation with the "other world," projects a this-worldly purpose independent of the question of each person's eternal salvation. For Calvin, this meant zeal for "the glory of God," or zeal for "sanctifying God's name," terms which are difficult to decipher from this point in time, but which, for Calvin, meant politics, moral striving, sharing in and helping to build human community—church, but also civil government.

At the conclusion of chapter 5 we discussed the church's call to explore the nature of its own grace-grounded community and the call to serve simultaneously the cause of community in the larger social order. Calvin defined this dual task in arguing that the civil government serves a purpose akin to that of the church, the purpose: "To adapt our manners to civil justice, to conciliate us to each other, to cherish common peace and tranquility. All these I confess to be superfluous, if the kingdom of God, as it now exists within us, extinguishes the present life." Calvin underlined the importance of this dual (civil and spiritual) resolve by describing the office of civil magistrate as a station, a calling, "not only sacred and lawful, but the most sacred, and by far the most honorable, . . . in mortal life."[11]

The course by which Calvin came to this affirmation of this-worldly social-political responsibility is difficult to track, but it seems to be an outgrowth of a teaching, a word, from Martin Bucer on the nature of the pastoral calling.[12] Early in his reforming career, before publication of the *Institutes* (1536) and before Geneva and William Farel, Calvin read the Strasbourg reformer's small classic, *Instruction in Christian Love* (1523). In that work, Bucer cited the willingness of both Moses (Ex. 32:32) and Paul (Rom. 9:1–3) *to sacrifice their eternal salvation* for the well-being of their people. Bucer declared that "the community is more important than particular individuals."[13] On the basis of this "instruction" Calvin resolved his own vocational uncertainty and turned from scholar to pastor-reformer. Calvin, however, was nurtured in Luther's spiritual egalitarianism and thus made application of Bucer's precept to *all* Christians: what was true for the pastor was true also for the people. It was here that Calvin broke with the medieval preoccupation with eternal blessedness, and came to these words: "It certainly is the part of a Christian . . . to ascend higher than merely to seek and secure the salvation of his own soul." The "ascent higher" was the commitment in this temporal realm to human community, to the doing of a "will of God" freed up from a morose preoccupation with eternal salvation.[14]

Calvin subsequently expanded on this theme in connection with his description of the spiritual nature of the community of faith. Each believer, each individual, Calvin asserted, is possessed of a unique gift, a grace, which is not his or hers alone, but is given to the individual for the well-being, the upbuilding, of the community. Calvin wrote:

> [The clause] the "communion of saints," . . . though usually omitted by ancient writers, must not be overlooked, as it admirably expresses the quality of the church; just as if it had been said, *that saints are united in the fellowship of Christ on this condition, that all the blessings which God bestows upon them are mutually communicated to each other.* This, however, is not incompatible with a *diversity of graces,* for we know that the gifts of the Spirit are variously distributed.[15]

Calvin declared: "No member has its function for itself, or applies it for its own private use, but transfers it to its fellow members; nor does it derive any other advantage from it than that which it receives in common with the whole body. Thus, whatever the pious man can do, he is bound to do for his brethren, not consulting his own interest in any other way than by striving earnestly for the common edification of the church."[16]

This insight represents a remarkable individualization and communalization of a transcendent grace. For Calvin, justification, the gospel of grace in Christ, is inseparable from the communion of saints and undergirds it. The priesthood of all believers is experienced in the mutuality of shared gifts, the eagerness to be priest to one another, but also the openness to be ministered to by the other in faith. Elsewhere Calvin remarked:

> So long as we are pilgrims in the world faith is implicit, not only because as yet many things are hidden from us, but because involved in the mists of error, we attain not to all. The highest wisdom, even of him who has attained the greatest perfection, is to go forward, and endeavor in a calm and teachable spirit to make further progress. . . . God . . . [assigns] to each a measure of faith, that every teacher, however excellent, may still be disposed to learn.[17]

The mutuality in faith thus affirmed had, for Calvin, carryover significance for the political sphere. An aristocrat by disposition and upbringing, in a world fearful of anarchy (viz. Luther and the Peasants' Revolt, the concern about the Anabaptists), Calvin nonetheless moved in his political thought away from rule from above to embrace a form of government based upon mutual exchange among the many. Though he does not express it in quite these terms, he moved in the direction of an "openness to below," on the model of the church, schooled in a divine wisdom, a foolishness of God (1 Cor. 1:18–25) which is wiser than men and which challenges all established hierarchies. Calvin distrusted the concentration of political power in the hands of the few; and in line with the diversity of spiritual gifts, he anticipated the potential of such diversity also within the political order.[18]

> It very rarely happens that kings so rule themselves as never to dissent from what is just and right, or are possessed of so much acuteness and prudence as always to see correctly. Owing therefore to the vices or defects of men it is safer and more tolerable when several bear rule that they may thus mutually assist, instruct and admonish each other.[19]

It is worth noting that in line with the diversity of graces, the communal nature of spiritual gifts, Calvin came to view the injunction against women speaking in the church as a matter of custom, *not* divine ordinance. Jane Dempsey Douglass comments in *Women, Freedom, and Calvin:* "To the best of my present knowledge, Calvin is the only sixteenth-century theologian who views women's silence in church as an 'indifferent' matter, i.e., one determined by human rather than divine law."[20] One can deplore the fact that Calvin did not go further in this regard, but it was a step, a partial but important step, in affirmation of a transcendent spiritual grace which demands recognition of "voices," voices for all within the church. All are teachable by all in the communion of saints. Such a perception inevitably bore implications for the political order.

There is more. In a European political situation marked by the breakdown of the medieval social-religious order, major figures were concerned to shore up the political order. Luther himself strongly affirmed Romans 13:1–7, enjoining Christian obedience to the governing authorities. Calvin also embraced this classic scriptural text, but with a difference: he pointed up the fact that government came in a variety of forms, akin to the diversity of gifts in the church and, as indicated above, he expressed his preference for shared rule where mutuality in insight and admonition might obtain. This interpretation lent weight to the office of the "lesser magistrates" who had a duty to instruct and deter the "higher magistrates" when the latter failed in their responsibilities. Such, however, was not the distinctive source of Calvinist concern for politics; after all, Luther and the Saxon lawyers had earlier asserted the responsibilities of the "lesser magistrates."[21] What initiated subsequent Calvinist political activism was Calvin's "third use" of the law which went beyond Luther's *two* uses (restraint of evil, conviction of the conscience). For Calvin law possessed a positive, creative role in shaping the life of a people, in defining a social goal that could bring glory to God. Calvin wrote, "The third use of the law (being also the principal use . . .) has respect to believers in whose hearts the spirit of God already flourishes and reigns." The law, Calvin asserts, "does not now perform toward us the part of a hard taskmaster, . . . but in the perfection to which it exhorts us, points out the goal at which, during the whole course of our lives, it is not less our interest than our duty to aim."[22]

Calvin argued that morality is not a means to salvation, but a means, within the framework of community, of honoring God. Morality serves not an otherworldly goal (eternal salvation) but a this-worldly one—in which the life of the community is given priority. While not likely to assuage modern apprehensions about "moralism," Calvin's enlistment of believers in a common calling laid the basis for an obedience to God which precluded simple acquiescence in inherited patterns of civic passivity. With the third use of the law, political responsibility for correction and redress shifted from the lesser magistrates to the people. Romans 13 was joined, politically, to the injunction to "obey God rather than men" (Acts 5:29). And then came Calvin's final injunction:

> And that our courage may not fail, Paul stimulates us by the additional consideration (I Cor. 7:23) that we were redeemed by Christ at the great price which our redemption cost him, in order that we might not yield a slavish obedience to the depraved wishes of men, far less do homage to their impiety.[23]

That we have here a lived understanding of the faith is clear from two brief, subsequent historical profiles. In 1630, almost a century after Calvin's letter to Sadoleto, John Winthrop, a layman, preached to a company of men, women, and children, to families, on a voyage to Massachusetts:

> We must entertaine each other in brotherly affeccion, wee must be willing to abridge ourselves of our superfluities, for the supply of others necessities, wee must uphold a familiar Commerce together in all meekenes, gentlenes, patience and liberality, we must delight in eache other, make others condicions our own, rejoyce together, mourne together, labour, and suffer together, always haveing before our eyes our Commission and Community in the worke, our Community as members of the same body; soe shall wee keep the unitie of the spirit in the bond of peace, the Lord will be our God and delight to dwell among us . . . so that we shall see much more of his wisdome, power, goodness and truthe than formerly wee have been acquainted with . . . that men shall say of succeeding plantacions: the Lord make it like that of New England; for wee must consider that wee shall be as a City upon a hill.[24]

The Puritan image of building "a City upon a hill" expressed the essence of Christian duty, *a response to a redemption already declared and accepted,* which in turn stimulated common effort and sacrifice to make manifest God's grace and glory. As Winthrop described it: "The worke . . . [was] to seeke out a place of Cohabitation and Consortshipp under a due form of government both civill and ecclesiasticall. In such case as this the care of the publique must oversway all private respects, by which not only conscience, but meare Civill policy doth bind us."[25]

Then from more recent times in Europe, a second profile is drawn. In the early 1930s, in Germany, a relative handful of Christians fought to preserve Christian life and community against the expansive claims of National Socialism. Karl Barth, as is generally known, was a leading theological figure in this struggle. In 1933 when informed by a younger colleague, Dietrich Bonhoeffer, that the latter had left his duties in Berlin to take over the pastoral responsibilities of two German-speaking congregations in London, Barth offered a rebuke. I quote the rebuke at length, for it states well the challenge of faith:

> Look, I gladly suppose . . . that this departure was personally necessary for you! But I must be allowed to add, "What does even 'personal necessity' mean at the present moment!" I think that I can see from your letter that you like all of us—yes, like all of us!—are suffering under the quite uncommon difficulty of taking "certain steps" in the present chaos. But should it not dawn on you that that is no reason for withdrawing from this chaos, that we are rather required in and with our uncertainty . . . to do our bit . . . ? I just will not allow you to put such a private tragedy on the stage in view of what is at stake for the German church today, as though

there were not time afterwards, . . . for the study of the different complexes and inhibitions from which you suffer, as indeed others also must. No, to all the reasons or excuses which you might perhaps still be able to put in front of me, I will give only one answer: "And the German church?" "And the German church?"—until you are back again in Berlin to attend faithfully and bravely to the [duties] which you have left behind there. . . . One simply cannot become weary just now. Still less can one go to England! What in all the world would you want to do there? . . . You must now leave go of all these intellectual flourishes and special considerations, however interesting they may be, and think of only one thing, that you are a German, that the house of your church is on fire, that you know enough and can say what you know well enough to be able to help and that you must return to your post by the next ship. As things are, shall we say the ship after next?[26]

There are echoes in Barth's rebuke of the young Bonhoeffer of the young Calvin's rebuke to the older Cardinal Sadoleto. Personal concerns—for eternal salvation or of self-doubt—cannot be given priority in the determination of Christian responsibility. At some point, perhaps many points, ultimate trust in God's grace must be affirmed and the doing of the will of God must be pressed in each situation of responsibility.

For Barth, in the early Hitler years, the will of God was defined as a defense of the freedom of the church to be the church and resistance to the idolatry of National Socialism. At a later time Barth offered criticism of the church's too-narrow focus on the defense of its own life. In 1935 he criticized the Confessing Church—and himself as well—with the following words: "She has fought hard to a certain extent for the freedom and purity of her proclamation, but she has, for instance, remained silent on the action against the Jews, on the amazing treatment of political opponents, on the suppression of the freedom of the press in the new Germany and on so much else against which the Old Testament prophets would certainly have spoken out."[27] And then in 1946, with the end of the war, in a discussion of "The Christian Community and the Civil Community," Barth argued for the inseparability of the church's concern for its own life from concern for the condition of all people, beyond race and creed, within the bounds of the state.

The Church desires that the shape and reality of the State in this fleeting world should point towards the Kingdom of God, not away from it. Its desire is not that human politics should cross the politics of God, but that they should proceed, however distantly, on parallel lines. . . . [The Church's] . . . political activity is therefore a profession of its Christian faith. By its political activity it calls the State from neutrality . . . into co-responsibility before God, thereby remaining faithful to its own particular mission.[28]

Barth's view of the state's "co-responsibility before God" presupposed the existence of a secular state. The state did not need to see itself responsible "before God" but responsible only for a humane life for its citizenry. Just as the church, in the context of a transcendent grace, affirms in its own life the freedom, responsibility, and participation of all its people, so it will want and "stand for the equality and responsibility of all . . . citizens. . . . It will stand for their equality before the law that unites and binds them all, for their equality in working together to establish and carry out the law." This freedom and participation of the citizenry must not be abridged by "differences of religious belief or unbelief," class, race, or gender.[29]

Those who have not read Calvin will, of course, not recognize the source of this argument.[30] Barth has purged Calvin of the ghost of "Christendom," of "political theocracy," in which the state is seen as having a special responsibility to serve the church. Rather, Barth sees in Calvin the potential recognition of a secular and neutral state[31] without infringement of Calvin's basic insight that "political activity is . . . a profession of . . . Christian faith."

And what does this theological dialogue with the past yield in the context of our analysis of progress and technology? It comes to this. Calvin proposes that Christian faith is the communal affirmation of a transcendent grace which is grounded in God, a Reigning Freedom and Purpose, which gives rise to a this-worldly human freedom and purpose.

This freedom and purpose makes community a prime goal of Christian striving—to the glory of God and the fulfilling of human promise. With this understanding of Christian vocation the community of faith—*in our time*—must recognize the historical actuality that technology has departed from the purpose of community building and now serves mainly its own purposes, and those of corporate profit. "Progress" once had a goal in human community; but technology has now claimed "progress" for itself and is leading the community ever closer to global death. It does this by pursuing its own distinctive innovative purposes and by assigning to society responsibility for failure to use properly its varied gifts. But in fact the community, society, is often the victim of these very gifts since the social impact of a new technology is most frequently realized long after the particular technology has been established. Meanwhile, the corporate-technological complex moves on to introduce ever new innovations in pursuit of economic advantage and power. Most new technologies are easily salable precisely at this point: their future costs are never clear at their introduction. The broad populace has naively come to believe that technological novelty is identical with progress. In political terms this process has become a subtle form of tyranny, a tyranny of the technological-economic "future" which more and more saps political structures of their autonomy and their present purpose of building community. There are variations on this history among the different nations, but in the main this is the pattern, the pattern that has simultaneously introduced the world-wide ecological crisis. It goes without saying that the present level of world population is dependent on many of the technologies now in place, but this level, and its continued high rate of increase, portends environmental disaster at the same time that it contributes to the decline of social-political meaning.[32]

Disillusion with social-political promise has had its own role to play in this history—a phenomenon for which technology is *not* chiefly responsible. The political age, which has encompassed the French and Russian revolutions down to our own time, has come to an end. The history of disillusion has deprived utopian political ideologies of their past allure. These former visions of future human felicity, which once commanded historical commitment and sacrifice, have waned—drained of appeal by disillusion. The sorry and frightful state of Marxism in our time is testimony to this reality. It is a frightful thing because its collapse is feeding new, perhaps threatening, parochialisms and because Marxism once served to check, in the West, myopic exploitative excesses.

At this point, the spiritual insights of Calvin lend instruction, especially in the face of such large-scale social-political disillusion. Unlike Moltmann, whose emphasis upon hope and a future that constantly claims the present was discussed in chapter 5, Calvin spoke of a "past" redemption and a commitment and morality free from obsession with future "rewards," a commitment and morality that spends itself "foolishly" on the impossible goal of social healing and transformation. Calvin called for a "perseverance of the saints," beyond disillusion, fixed on the will of God. Its morality, its commitment to community, is "free gift" back to God, an "obedience" beyond reward. Whereas a natural, secular hope of fulfilling communal existence falters in our time, a Christian "otherworldly this-worldliness" persists. "That our courage may not fail, Paul stimulates us by the . . . consideration . . . that we were redeemed by Christ at the great price which our redemption cost him."[33]

The community of faith certainly joins in the present growing concern for the environment and the efforts to preserve the natural order. A new "political" purpose is building—that of preserving life itself. This concern is dictating a politically potent activity and morality that demand a more responsive government. The realization is spreading that the "old order," dominated by business interests and growth economics, leads to death; the *ancien régime* of our time is coming under assault by articulate critics and groups that scorn its excesses. Corporate enterprise, "business as usual," the furthering of a vacuous technology, can no longer assume acquiescence by an uninformed public. Awareness rises that people need not, *ought* not, subsidize economic enterprise with life and health, that clean air, clean water, are rights, natural and human, which must be asserted. Day by day comes the realization that our blue, beautiful, cloud-flecked miracle in space is now haunted by death. This is a situation in which we all have played a part, as we have indulged ourselves in our comforts and technological distractions. Now the question is asked, What does a footprint on the moon mean against the backdrop of a ravaged, dying earth?

At this point the community of faith joins in a threefold task: (1) It struggles, in league with friends from secular and other religious paths of life, to preserve the natural order, God's earth. (2) It seeks more fully to realize its peculiar calling as a community of grace, beyond inherited privilege, race, gender. (3) It endeavors, equally ardently, to keep open and further the structures of speech and participation that exist in the political realm. Only an intensification of social-political meaning can counterbalance the forthcoming restrictions on economic exploitation of the natural order. Faith's vision cannot be fixed on the next life, though that prospect is not denied. Rather, the responsibility and joy of faith are set in this life—in pursuing God's will for human community and in praise of God for a healing already accomplished. To abridge such purpose, wantonly or passively, is no service of God. Rather the call stands:

> You are the light of the world. A city set on a hill cannot be hid.
>   (Matthew 5:14)

A green, a verdant, hill is part of this vision and task, part of this ongoing, historical praise of God.

NOTES

Preface

1. Lewis Spitz, ed., *The Reformation: Basic Interpretations* (Lexington, Mass.: D. C. Heath & Co., 1972), pp. 34–35.
2. The 1989 image of the *Exxon Valdez* is no doubt also etched in our memories, but I believe this event is qualitatively different from the Chernobyl and Challenger events in that the latter two were viewed as bearers of promise for the future, a dimension much less apparent in the *Exxon Valdez* affair, despite the environmental threat it also clearly poses.

Chapter 1: Has Technology Become Our History?

1. More than twenty-five years ago Geoffrey Barraclough, in *An Introduction to Contemporary History* (New York: Basic Books, 1964), anticipated in a most perceptive way the impact of scientific technology on world history; see esp. pp. 36–58.
2. Langdon Winner has made this the theme of inquiry in relation to political thought. See Langdon Winner, *Autonomous Technology: Technics-Out-of-Control as a Theme in Political Thought* (Cambridge, Mass.: MIT Press, 1977).
3. See ch. 5 below for a discussion of Tillich's theology in relation to technology. It can be noted in passing that the romantic spirit figures large in the thought of both Tillich and Whitehead. But in technology, I will argue, we have the opposite of romanticism—we are increasingly attuned to and constrained by our own human creation.
4. Carl Becker, *The Heavenly City of the Eighteenth-Century Philosophers* (New Haven, Conn.: Yale University Press, 1932), p. 17.
5. Ibid., pp. 18–19.
6. This is not to say that what is called "pure science" does not continue to attract and enthrall. It does. Whereas earlier science stirred hopes of social and political advance it hardly serves that purpose any longer.

7. Ronald W. Clark, *The Greatest Power on Earth* (New York: Harper & Row, 1980), pp. 291–292.

8. Ibid., p. 292.

9. *New York Times*, Sept. 23, 1986, p. A1:6.

10. Ibid., p. C6:3.

11. Ibid., p. C6:5, 6.

12. Ibid., p. C6:4.

13. *New York Times,* Aug. 22, 1986, pp. A1, A4.

14. Ibid., p. A4:6.

15. Ibid., p. A4:1.

16. *New York Times,* Nov. 6, 1986, p. A26:1.

17. Marshall I. Goldman, "Keeping the Cold War Out of Chernobyl," *Technology Review*, vol. 89 (July 1986), p. 18.

18. C. Hohenemser et al., "Chernobyl: An Early Report," *Environment*, vol. 28 (June 1986), p. 9. This article represents one of the earliest scientific assessments of the damage caused by Chernobyl and stands, even after the final Soviet report, as an especially instructive analysis.

19. Ibid., p. 11.

20. *New York Times*, Sept. 23, 1986, p. C6:5.

21. *New York Times,* Aug. 22, 1986, p. A4:1.

22. Goldman, "Keeping the Cold War Out of Chernobyl," p. 18.

23. Ibid.

24. *New York Times*, Oct. 27, 1986, p. A1:1, 2.

25. Goldman, "Keeping the Cold War Out of Chernobyl," p. 19.

26. Robert Jay Lifton, *Death and Life: Survivors of Hiroshima* (1967; reprint, New York: Basic Books, 1982).

27. *Minneapolis Star and Tribune*, May 23, 1986, p. 17A. For a further account of the arbitrary and unexpected nature of the danger of radioactive fallout, see C. Hohenemser et al., "Chernobyl."

28. *New York Times,* June 16, 1986, pp. A1:3, A10:2.

29. See Tom Wolfe, "Everyman vs. Astropower," *Newsweek*, Feb. 10, 1986, pp. 40–41.

30. *New York Times,* Feb. 2, 1986, p. A18:1.

31. *New York Times,* Feb. 24, 1986, p. A1:3.

32. *New York Times,* June 10, 1986, p. A1:6.

33. *New York Times,* March 4, 1986, p. C5:1.

34. *New York Times,* June 11, 1986, p. B6:1.

35. *New York Times,* Feb. 2, 1986, p. A34:1, 2.

36. *New York Times,* Aug. 22, 1986, p. A4:6 (emphasis mine).

37. *New York Times,* Aug. 28, 1984, p. A1:6.

38. *A Nation at Risk: The Imperative for Educational Reform,* Report of the National Commission on Excellence in Education, Washington, D.C., April 1983, p. 5.

39. *New York Times,* May 5, 1983, p. A1:1.

40. *A Nation at Risk,* p. 5. I am indebted to Professor Ted Mitchell of the Education Department of Dartmouth College for pointing out the military nature of this language.

41. *New York Times,* Aug. 26, 1984, p. C3:5.
42. *New York Times,* Feb. 8, 1986, p. A17:1.
43. The consulting firm was Berman-Weiler Associates of Berkeley, California. Prior to the Minnesota study the firm had established a reputation for its interest in voucher programs.
44. Paul Berman et al., *The Minnesota Plan,* vol. 1 (Berkeley, Calif.: B. W. Associates, 1984), pp. iii, 1–3, 66.
45. Ibid., p. 3.
46. This was accomplished in November 1986. A compromise was struck and open enrollment was proposed as optional for local school districts. One of the expected results of this development is an increased need for competing school districts to establish public relations and recruitment offices. *Minneapolis Star and Tribune,* Feb. 1, 1987, p. A1:1.
47. The suggestion that Minnesota could make do with less "advanced higher education" is also found in the Minnesota Business Partnership report, Berman, *Minnesota Plan,* vol. 1, p. 79. For details of the 25 percent enrollment cut, see the *Minneapolis Star and Tribune,* Feb. 7, 1987, p. B4.
48. Lawrence A. Cremin, *American Education: The National Experience, 1783–1876* (New York: Harper & Row, 1980).
49. See Lawrence A. Cremin, *The American Common School: An Historic Conception* (New York: Bureau of Publications, Teachers College, Columbia University, 1951), pp. 29–33.
50. Cremin, *American Education,* p. 138.
51. Horace Mann, quoted in ibid., pp. 140–141.
52. Professor Edith MacMullen of Yale University has suggested this symbolism.

Chapter 2: Technology and the Idea of Progress

1. See Lawrence Cremin, *The American Common School: An Historic Conception* (New York: Bureau of Publications, Teachers College, Columbia University, 1951), pp. 69–70, 192.
2. Horace Mann, quoted by Lawrence A. Cremin, *American Education: The National Experience, 1783–1876* (New York: Harper & Row, 1980), p. 138.
3. The economic interpretation of the Constitution and American history, as expressed for example in the work of the historian Charles Beard, is important but not overridingly so, a point to be argued in broader terms in this chapter.
4. Cremin, *American Education,* pp. 138–139.
5. John F. Kasson, *Civilizing the Machine: Technology and Republican Values in America, 1776–1900* (New York: Penguin Books, 1977), pp. 22–36.
6. Ibid., p. 234. Kasson does not spell out what these "new political strategies" and "categories of value" were or are to be.
7. James Michener, the novelist, writes in this vein two days after the Challenger disaster. See James Michener, "Death in Pursuit of Our Time's Prime Adventure," *Minneapolis Star and Tribune,* Jan. 30, 1986, p. 13A:1.
8. In a review of Bury's book in 1920, Carl Becker notes the peculiarity of this late attention to such a dominant idea.

9. J. B. Bury, *The Idea of Progress* (London: Macmillan & Co., 1920), p. 5.
10. Ibid., pp. 10–11.
11. Ibid., pp. 22–23.
12. Ibid., p. 30.
13. Ibid.
14. Ibid., p. 109.
15. Ibid., p. 141.
16. Ibid., p. 164.
17. Ibid., pp. 175, 176.
18. Ibid., pp. 220, 221.
19. Ibid., pp. 209, 211.
20. Ibid., p. 214.
21. Ibid., p. 293.
22. Ibid., p. 290.
23. Ibid., p. 330.
24. Ibid., pp. 332–333.
25. Ibid., pp. 335, 336.
26. Ibid., p. 337.
27. Ibid., p. 347.
28. Ibid., pp. 348–349.
29. For example, the reviewer for the *Times Literary Supplement*, June 10, 1920, p. 1, comments: "If the history of an idea is to have all its interest and value, it requires a criticism of the idea itself as well as its story, and needs to be written by one who is as much a thinker as an historian." Cf. also the *American Historical Review*, vol. 26 (October 1920), p. 78.
30. Bury, *Idea of Progress*, p. 21.
31. On this point it is somewhat surprising that Owen Chadwick, in his otherwise notable book *The Secularization of the European Mind* (Cambridge: Cambridge University Press, 1974), should so seriously neglect the idea of Progress in describing the "secularization" of the nineteenth-century European mind.
32. John Baillie, *The Belief in Progress* (New York: Charles Scribner's Sons, 1951), p. 104.
33. Franklin Le Van Baumer, *Main Currents of Western Thought* (New York: Alfred A. Knopf, 1954), p. 698.
34. Robert Nisbet, *History of the Idea of Progress* (New York: Basic Books, 1980), p. 11.
35. Cf. ibid., pp. 25–27; cf. Ludwig Edelstein, *The Idea of Progress in Classical Antiquity* (Baltimore: Johns Hopkins Press, 1967), pp. 32–33.
36. M. I. Finley, "Up from Democritus," *New York Review of Books*, June 20, 1968, pp. 36, 37.
37. Nisbet, *History of the Idea of Progress*, p. 47.
38. Ibid., pp. 313–316.
39. Ibid., pp. 102–103.
40. Ibid., p. 102.
41. Ibid., pp. 105, 106.
42. This is not to say that there is not a continuing problem in the relation of

ethical commitments and definitions of meaning in history; cf. Hayden White, *Metahistory, The Historical Imagination in Nineteenth-Century Europe* (Baltimore: Johns Hopkins University Press, 1973).

43. *New York Times Book Review*, March 16, 1980, p. 4.

44. J. M. Cameron, "Sounding Off," *New York Review of Books*, April 17, 1980, p. 36.

45. Ibid., p. 38.

46. Ibid.

47. George G. Iggers, "The Idea of Progress in Historiography and Social Thought Since the Enlightenment," in Gabriel A. Almond, Marvin Chodorow, and Roy Harvey Pearce, eds., *Progress and Its Discontents* (Berkeley, Calif.: University of California Press, 1982), pp. 41–66.

48. Ibid., p. 43.

49. Ibid., pp. 43, 45.

50. See A. W. H. Adkins, *Moral Values and Political Behavior in Ancient Greece* (New York: W. W. Norton & Co., 1972), and C. M. Bowra, *The Greek Experience* (New York: New American Library of World Literature, 1957).

51. See n. 32 above.

52. Karl Lowith, *Meaning in History* (Chicago: University of Chicago Press, 1949).

53. E.g., ibid., pp. 202–203; Reinhold Niebuhr, *Faith and History* (New York: Charles Scribner's Sons, 1949), pp. 205–213; see also Norman Cohn, *The Pursuit of the Millennium* (London: Oxford University Press, 1957).

54. Johan Huizinga, in his classic 1924 study *The Waning of the Middle Ages* (New York: Doubleday & Co., Anchor Books, 1954), has given full and convincing statement of this.

55. See Paul Tillich, *The Courage to Be* (New Haven, Conn.: Yale University Press, 1952). For further discussion of this point, see ch. 5, n. 18 below.

56. Baumer, *Main Currents of Western Thought*, p. 109.

57. A. Richard Reed, "The Expansion of Europe," in *The Meaning of the Renaissance and Reformation*, ed. Richard L. DeMolen (Boston: Houghton Mifflin Co., 1974), pp. 315–320.

58. See especially the article by Lynn White, Jr., "What Accelerated Technological Progress in the Western Middle Ages?" in *Scientific Change*, ed. A. C. Crombie (New York: Basic Books, 1963), pp. 272–291; also Lynn White, Jr., *Medieval Religion and Technology* (Berkeley, Calif.: University of California Press, 1974), pp. xi–xxiv.

59. Lynn White, Jr., *Medieval Religion and Technology*, p. xviii.

60. Lynn White, Jr., "What Accelerated Technological Progress?" In this article White attempts to do for technology what Max Weber in 1904–05 attempted to do for the rise of capitalism; cf. Max Weber, *The Protestant Ethic and the Spirit of Capitalism* (1930; reprint, New York: Charles Scribner's Sons, 1958).

61. John M. Headley, "The Continental Reformation," in DeMolen, *Meaning of the Renaissance and Reformation*, pp. 162–163.

62. Michael Walzer, *The Revolution of the Saints: A Study in the Origins of Radical Politics* (New York: Atheneum Publishers, 1968).

63. For a brief account of the import and impact of the supernova of 1572, see

Arthur Koestler, *The Watershed* (Garden City, N.Y.: Doubleday & Co., Anchor Books, 1960), pp. 91–94.

64. Taken from the title of Copernicus' book *The Revolution of the Heavenly Bodies*.

65. See Stephen Toulmin and June Goodfield, *The Fabric of the Heavens* (New York: Harper & Row, Harper Torchbook, 1961), pp. 169–181.

66. J. Logie Robertson, ed., *The Complete Poetical Works of James Thomson* (London: Oxford University Press, 1908), pp. 436–437.

67. James B. Wood, "The Impact of the Wars of Religion: A View of France in 1581," *Sixteenth Century Journal,* vol. 15, no. 2 (Summer 1984), p. 167.

68. Ibid., p. 141.

69. Williston Walker, *A History of the Christian Church,* rev. ed. (New York: Charles Scribner's Sons, 1959), p. 396.

70. Voltaire, quoted by John Herman Randall, Jr., *The Making of the Modern Mind,* rev. ed. (Boston: Houghton Mifflin Co., 1940), p. 304.

71. Crane Brinton, ed., *The Portable Age of Reason Reader* (New York: Viking Press, 1956), pp. 226–227.

72. Ibid., p. 227.

73. Iggers, "The Idea of Progress in Historiography," in Almond, Chodorow, and Pearce, *Progress and Its Discontents,* p. 66.

Chapter 3: Disillusion and Power

1. Carl L. Becker, *The Heavenly City of the Eighteenth-Century Philosophers* (New Haven, Conn.: Yale University Press, 1932), pp. 29–30.

2. Ibid., pp. 30–31.

3. Ibid., pp. 39–40.

4. Ibid., pp. 40, 41.

5. See *Journal of Philosophy*, vol. 30 (March 30, 1933), p. 190.

6. *Times Literary Supplement,* Feb. 16, 1933, p. 104.

7. *American Historical Review,* vol. 38 (April 1933), pp. 590–591.

8. See Raymond O. Rockwood, ed., *Carl Becker's Heavenly City Revisited* (Ithaca, N.Y.: Cornell University Press, 1958).

9. One symposium participant, Louis Gottschalk, from the University of Chicago, noted Peter Gay's misperception; cf. ibid., pp. 89–95.

10. Becker, *Heavenly City,* pp. 102–103.

11. Rockwood, *Carl Becker's Heavenly City Revisited,* p. 51.

12. Becker, *Heavenly City,* p. 14. Though Gay accuses Becker of dependence upon Alfred North Whitehead for some of his basic categories, the cosmology described here was certainly not shared by Whitehead; cf. Rockwood, *Carl Becker's Heavenly City Revisited,* p. 31.

13. Becker, *Heavenly City,* p. 15.

14. Ibid., p. 158.

15. Ibid., pp. 160–161.

16. Carl Becker, *Progress and Power* (New York: Vintage Books, 1965), pp. 6–7.

17. See Franklin Le Van Baumer, *Main Currents of Western Thought* (New York: Alfred A. Knopf, 1954), pp. 577–585.

18. Paul Fussell, *The Great War and Modern Memory* (New York: Oxford University Press, 1975), p. 158.
19. Ibid., pp. 163–164.
20. Ibid., pp. 21–24.
21. Ernest Hemingway, quoted by Fussell, ibid., p. 21.
22. Gordon A. Craig, *Europe Since 1815* (New York: Holt, Rinehart & Winston, 1961), pp. 501–502.
23. Ibid., pp. 502–503.
24. Henry James, quoted by Fussell, *Great War*, p. 8.
25. Philip Gibbs, quoted by Fussell, ibid.
26. Becker, *Heavenly City,* pp. 166–167.
27. Ibid., p. 167.
28. Ibid., p. 168.
29. Ibid., p. 30 (see n. 1 above).
30. Ibid., p. 118.
31. Ibid., p. 102. It is, of course, true that the Homeric tradition in ancient Greece claimed a notable this-worldly goal, the pursuit of honor; and the Epicureans embraced friendship as the proper human quest.
32. Ibid., pp. 45–46.
33. See n. 28 above.
34. See n. 24 above.
35. See n. 25 above.
36. Becker, *Progress and Power,* pp. 24–25.
37. Ibid., pp. 27–31.
38. Ibid., p. 26. Jacob Bronowski, in *The Ascent of Man* (Boston: Little, Brown & Co., 1974), gives priority to the hand tool, the development of the brain following the technological advance. Bronowski argues that "the hand is the cutting edge of the mind."
39. Becker, *Progress and Power*, pp. 87–94.
40. Ibid., pp. 113–114.
41. Cf. John Archibald Wheeler, "The Universe as Home for Man," *American Scientist*, vol. 62 (1974), pp. 683–691; also J. A. Wheeler, "Genesis and Observership" in *Proceedings of the 5th International Congress on Logic, Methodology and Philosophy of Science*, ed. R. E. Butts and J. Hintikka, 2 (Dordrecht, Holland: D. Reidel Publishing Co., 1977), pp. 3–33.
42. Becker, *Progress and Power,* pp. 96–97.
43. Ibid., pp. 97–98.
44. Ibid., pp. 98, 107.
45. Ibid., p. 104. Becker identifies here the problem more fully elaborated forty years later by Alvin Toffler in *Future Shock* (New York: Random House, 1970).
46. Becker, *Progress and Power*, pp. 105, 107.
47. Ibid., pp. 106, 107.
48. Ibid., pp. 107, 108.
49. Ibid., pp. 108–109.
50. Ibid., p. 109.
51. Ibid., pp. 111–112.

52. Thomas S. Kuhn, *The Structure of Scientific Revolutions* (Chicago: University of Chicago Press, 1962).
53. Albert Einstein anticipated this development in his break with positivism and Ernst Mach in the 1920s. Cf. Gerald Holton, *Thematic Origins of Scientific Thought* (Cambridge, Mass.: Harvard University Press, 1973), pp. 197–257. For a popular rendering of more recent developments, see the 1985 Nova film *What Einstein Never Knew.*
54. The 1980 documentary film on the life of Robert Oppenheimer, *The Day After Trinity,* helps to tell this story in a profound way. Further discussion of the role of the scientific community in the fashioning of the atomic bomb follows in chapter 4.
55. See B. F. Skinner, *Walden Two* (New York: Macmillan Co., 1948) and *Beyond Freedom and Dignity* (New York: Alfred A. Knopf, 1971).
56. Becker, *Progress and Power,* pp. 108–109 (see n. 49 above).
57. Marshall McLuhan, *Understanding Media* (New York: McGraw-Hill Book Co., 1964).
58. Seymour Papert, *Mindstorms: Children, Computers, and Powerful Ideas* (New York: Basic Books, 1980), pp. 212–213.
59. Sherry Turkle, *The Second Self: Computers and the Human Spirit* (New York: Simon & Schuster, 1984); also Theodore Roszak, *The Cult of Information* (New York: Pantheon Books, 1986), pp. 47–86.
60. Langdon Winner, *Autonomous Technology: Technics-Out-of-Control as a Theme in Political Thought* (Cambridge, Mass.: MIT Press, 1977).
61. See ibid., p. 14; see also Raymond Aron, *Progress and Disillusion* (New York: Praeger Publishers, 1968), p. 214.
62. Alvin Toffler, *The Third Wave* (New York: William Morrow & Co., 1980).
63. Becker, *Progress and Power,* p. 107.
64. Melvin Kranzberg and Carroll W. Pursell, Jr., eds., *Technology in Western Civilization,* vol. 1 (New York: Oxford University Press, 1967), p. 325.
65. Lewis Mumford, *Technics and Civilization* (New York: Harcourt, Brace & Co., 1934), p. 132.
66. See above, pp. 50–52.
67. Karl Polanyi has persuasively argued this point in *The Great Transformation* (New York: Rinehart & Co., 1944).
68. *Minneapolis Star and Tribune,* May 3, 1987, p. 29A.
69. Winner, *Autonomous Technology,* p. 89.
70. Leo Marx has recently written in a vein parallel to what has been argued in this chapter; see Leo Marx, "Does Improved Technology Mean Progress?", *Technology and the Future,* ed. Albert H. Teich (New York: St. Martin's Press, 1990).

Chapter 4: Technology and Values

1. Werner Heisenberg, *Physics and Beyond, Encounters and Conversations* (New York: Harper & Row, 1971), p. 193.
2. Ibid., pp. 195–196.
3. Ibid., p. 195. This, however, is not a convincing argument when one considers the intense competition among individual scientists for the "immortality"

and acclaim that comes with every new scientific discovery; cf. Jerry Gaston, *Originality and Competition in Science* (Chicago: University of Chicago Press, 1973), pp. 71–74.

4. Jacob Bronowski, *Science and Human Values* (New York: Harper & Brothers, Harper Torchbook, 1959), pp. 34, 70–71.

5. Ibid., p. 68.

6. Ibid., p. 70.

7. Ibid., p. xiii.

8. See especially Diana Crane, *Invisible Colleges: Diffusion of Knowledge in Scientific Communities* (Chicago: University of Chicago Press, 1972), and Gaston, *Originality and Competition.*

9. Though no philosopher of science, Jacques Ellul comes close to Bronowski on this point. Cf. Jacques Ellul, *The Technological System* (New York: Continuum, 1980), pp. 127–130. See also Langdon Winner, *Autonomous Technology* (Cambridge, Mass.: MIT Press, 1977), p. 63.

10. Bronowski, *Science and Human Values*, p. 7.

11. D. S. L. Cardwell, *Turning Points in Western Technology* (New York: Science History Publications, 1972), p. 100.

12. See A. B. Musson, ed., *Science, Technology, and Economic Growth in the Eighteenth Century* (London: Methuen, 1972), esp. Peter Mathis, "Who Unbound Prometheus? Science and Technical Change, 1600–1800," pp. 69–96.

13. For other discussions of this theme coming out of the scientific community after World War II, see James B. Conant, *Modern Science and Modern Man* (New York: Columbia University Press, 1952); Bertrand Russell, *The Impact of Science on Society* (New York: Columbia University Press, 1959); C. P. Snow, *The Two Cultures* (Cambridge: Cambridge University Press, 1959); Vannevar Bush, *Science Is Not Enough* (New York: William Morrow & Co., 1967).

14. See above, pp. 51–52.

15. Freeman Dyson, the mathematician-physicist, who knows intimately the worlds of both pure science and applied science (technology), calls attention to some of these characteristics; cf. Freeman Dyson, *Disturbing the Universe* (New York: Harper & Row, 1979), pp. 51, 72–77, 114.

16. Bronowski, *Science and Human Values*, p. 68.

17. Lynn White, Jr., "What Accelerated Technological Progress in the Western Middle Ages?" in *Scientific Change,* ed. A. C. Crombie (New York: Basic Books, 1963), pp. 286–287.

18. Ibid., p. 285.

19. See Max Weber, *The Protestant Ethic and the Spirit of Capitalism* (1930; reprint, New York: Charles Scribner's Sons, 1958). For further discussion of this point, see ch. 6, n. 9 below.

20. *Bacon's Advancement of Learning and The New Atlantis,* with preface by Thomas Case (London: Oxford University Press, 1906), p. 37 (1.5.6).

21. Francis Bacon, *The New Organon,* ed. Fulton H. Anderson (Indianapolis: Bobbs-Merrill Co., 1960), p. 58; see also p. 112.

22. The dedication of the *Novum Organum* to James I and his later description

of Solomon's "House of Learning" in the *New Atlantis* warrant such an assumption.

23. For a helpful discussion of Bacon, see Gary Bruce Deason, *The Philosophy of a Lord Chancellor: Religion, Science, and Social Stability in the World of Francis Bacon* (Ann Arbor, Mich.: University Microfilm International, 1978). Deason's work raises some question on his interpretation of the Reformation. He suggests that the egalitarianism of the Reformation is somehow grounded in the idea of the comprehensibility of scripture (see ibid., pp. 294–297). But in Luther and Calvin, the egalitarian theme is grounded in the message itself and not primarily in its scriptural form. Literacy was not the presupposition of the priesthood of all believers, justification by faith was. Literacy was only a second or third order of business compared to the *preached* word of grace.

24. This is especially clear in a Bacon essay/pamphlet, published in 1641, fifteen years after his death. Entitled *A Wise and Moderate Discourse Concerning Church Affaires*, the essay spells out Bacon's conservative political, ecclesiastical views. Bacon saw the destabilizing of the ecclesiastical order as a threat to the political order—and in this sphere he very much curtailed his egalitarian sentiments. Bacon's final advice on church reform was: "Lastly, whatsoever is pretended, the people is no meet judge or arbitrator; but rather the moderate, quiet, and private assemblies of the learned." Francis Bacon, *A Wise and Moderate Discourse Concerning Church Affaires,* 1641 (Puritan Collection, Speer Library, Princeton Theological Seminary), p. 46.

25. The work of Michael Walzer *The Revolution of the Saints* (New York: Atheneum Publishers, 1968) makes this point especially clear.

26. Bacon, *New Organon*, p. 114 (sec. 124).

27. Edwin T. Layton, Jr., *The Revolt of the Engineers* (Cleveland: Press of Case Western Reserve University, 1971), p. 55.

28. Samuel Lilley, *Men, Machines and History* (London: Cobbett Press, 1948), p. 26.

29. Ibid.

30. Scientific American, *Scientific Technology and Social Change* (New York: W. H. Freeman & Co., 1974), p. 55.

31. Hazel Henderson, "Information and the New Movements for Citizen Participation," *The Information Revolution,* special issue of *Annals of the American Academy of Political and Social Science*, March 1974.

32. For a brief summary of political assessments in this area, see Judith C. Perrolle, *Computers and Social Change: Information, Property, and Power* (Belmont, Calif.: Wadsworth Publishing Co., 1987), pp. 218–221.

33. Ibid., p. 219.

34. For comment on the overselling of the computer within the American business community, see Theodore Roszak, *The Cult of Information* (New York: Pantheon Books, 1986), esp. pp. 21–24; see also "Revving Up the American Factory," *New York Times*, Jan. 11, 1987, p. C1:3ff.

35. Daniel J. Boorstin, *The Republic of Technology: Reflections of Our Future Community* (New York: Harper & Row, 1978), p. 28.

36. Ibid., p. 29. Some question has to be raised with this simplistic assertion by

Boorstin. Is it in fact the case that a society can return to the order that existed before a revolution, e.g., the French Revolution? Cf. Hannah Arendt, *On Revolution* (New York: Viking Press, 1965), p. 49: "It was the French and not the American Revolution that set the world on fire, and it was consequently from the course of the French Revolution and not from the course of events in America . . . that our present use of the word 'revolution' received its connotations and overtones everywhere." More striking, the French philosopher-historian Henri Gouhier said of the same French Revolution: "The Revolution had something final about it. Whatever view one might hold regarding men and institutions, no counter-revolution was historically conceivable; any attempt to hark back to 1788 would have been absurd." Guy B. Metraux and Francis Crouzet, *The Nineteenth Century World* (New York: New American Library of World Literature, Mentor Books, 1963), p. 467.

37. Boorstin, *Republic of Technology*, p. 29.
38. Ibid., p. 30.
39. Ibid., p. 31.
40. Ibid., p. 49.
41. Ibid., p. 54.
42. Ibid., pp..56–57, 59.
43. For a critical review of Boorstin's book, see R. A. Sokolov's assessment in the *New York Times Book Review*, Aug. 6, 1978, p. 16.
44. Lewis Mumford, *Technics and Civilization* (New York: Harcourt, Brace & Co., 1934), see esp. pp. 368–373, 433–435.
45. Lewis Mumford, *The Myth of the Machine: Technics and Human Development* (New York: Harcourt, Brace & World, 1966), p. 9.
46. Ibid., p. 12.
47. Lewis Mumford, "Authoritarian and Democratic Technics," *Technology and Culture,* vol. 5, no. 1 (Winter 1964), pp. 2–3.
48. Ibid., p. 3.
49. Ibid., pp. 5–6. Jacques Ellul's analyses of the modern "technological society" and "technological system" very much coincide with this Mumford assessment.
50. Ibid., p. 7.
51. Martin Buber, *I and Thou* (New York: Charles Scribner's Sons, 1958), p. 3.
52. Ibid., pp. 34, 8.
53. Ibid., p. 11.
54. Ibid., p. 33.
55. Ibid., pp. 74–86.
56. Jacques Ellul makes much of Kant's ends/means distinction in his assessment of the technological society; see Jacques Ellul, *The Technological Society* (New York: Alfred A. Knopf, 1964).
57. Buber, *I and Thou*, p. 5.
58. The thought of Jean-Paul Sartre makes this precise point; see Jean-Paul Sartre, *Existentialism and Human Emotions* (New York: Philosophical Library, 1957), pp. 9–51.
59. Boorstin, *Republic of Technology*, pp. 59–60.
60. Ibid., p. 48.

61. There are some parallels here with Herbert Marcuse's argument in *One Dimensional Man* (Boston: Beacon Press, 1964).
62. The reference here is to the important work of John P. Diggins, *The Lost Soul of American Politics* (Chicago: University of Chicago Press, 1984).

Chapter 5: Technology and Theology

1. See reference above, ch. 4, n. 17. See also White's 1958 article "Dynamo and Virgin Reconsidered," reprinted in Lynn White, Jr., *Machina Ex Deo: Essays in the Dynamism of Western Culture* (Cambridge, Mass.: MIT Press, 1968), pp. 67–73.
2. White, "What Accelerated Technological Progress in the Western Middle Ages?," p. 103.
3. "The Historical Roots of Our Ecological Crisis" first appeared in the March 10, 1967, issue of *Science* magazine and was reprinted in numerous anthologies, including White's own collection of essays, *Machina Ex Deo*.
4. See ch. 2 above.
5. Revised Standard Version (New York: Thomas Nelson & Sons, 1952). This verse was explicitly cited by White in "Continuing the Conversation," in *Western Man and Environmental Ethics*, ed. Ian Barbour (Reading, Mass.: Addison-Wesley Publishing Co., 1973), p. 60. See also Lynn White, "The Future of Compassion," *Ecumenical Review*, vol. 30, no. 2 (April 1978), pp. 105–106.
6. White, *Machina Ex Deo*, pp. 86, 93.
7. White addressed the problem of natural law only in passing in his 1967 discussion; see "Historical Roots" in *Machina Ex Deo*, pp. 88–89. On the long history and significance of natural law in Christian thought, see Ernst Troeltsch, *The Social Teachings of the Christian Churches* (1911; reprint, New York: Harper & Brothers, 1960).
8. Thomas S. Derr, "Religion's Responsibility for the Ecologic Crisis: An Argument Run Amok," *Worldview*, vol. 18, no. 1 (January 1975), p. 45.
9. See George R. Lucas and Thomas W. Ogletree, eds., *Lifeboat Ethics: Moral Dilemmas of World Hunger* (New York: Harper & Row, 1976).
10. Lewis Mumford, *The Myth of the Machine: Technics and Human Development* (New York: Harcourt, Brace & World, 1966), p. 12.
11. Ibid., p. 168.
12. Derr, "Religion's Responsibility," p. 45.
13. White, "What Accelerated Technological Progress in the Western Middle Ages?," p. 92.
14. White, *Machina Ex Deo*, p. 90.
15. Ibid., p. 93. And yet, three times in his "Historical Roots," pp. 77, 79, 80, White refers to an important phenomenon with which the religious tradition had little to do, the coalescence, in the mid-nineteenth century, of science and technology. White fails to address here a problem, a dynamism that is operating independent of a "religious" explanation/correction.
16. Harvey Cox, *The Secular City* (New York: Macmillan Co., 1965), pp. 17–36.
17. I say this with a qualification. The French economist, social analyst, and

theologian Jacques Ellul certainly has addressed this problem with vigor and force, if not always with helpful clarity and historical cogency. Cf. also Langdon Winner's appraisal of Ellul's contribution, *Autonomous Technology* (Cambridge, Mass.: MIT Press, 1977), p. 130.

18. Paul Tillich, *The Courage to Be* (New Haven, Conn.: Yale University Press, 1952), pp. 38–39, 53–59. See above, p. 47.

19. This theme and the main lines of Tillich's later system were laid out in an early work, *Mystik und Schuldbewusstsein in Schellings Philosophischer Entwicklung* (Gütersloh: Bertelsmann, 1912).

20. Tillich, *Courage to Be*, pp. 148, 164.

21. Charles W. Kegley and Robert W. Bretall, eds., *The Theology of Paul Tillich* (New York: Macmillan Co., 1952), p. 8.

22. Paul Tillich, *The Protestant Era* (Chicago: University of Chicago Press, 1948), pp. xiv–xv.

23. Tillich dedicated a 1924 work *Das System der Wissenschaften nach Gegenständen und Methoden* to the memory of Ernst Troeltsch. Troeltsch had argued that the ethos of the modern world was dominated by the principles of autonomy, this-worldliness, and the belief in progress; see Ernst Troeltsch, *Protestantism and Progress* (Boston: Beacon Press, 1958). Tillich was fully in accord with the first two of these principles, but also argued that Troeltsch's work and his tendency toward historical relativism needed correction with a metaphysical grounding; see Tillich, "Ernst Troeltsch: Der Historismus und seine Probleme," *Theologische Literaturzeitung*, vol. 49, no. 2 (1924).

24. This, of course, was offered with the qualification that God's creativity is infinite and provides the possibility of finite creativity; cf. Paul Tillich, *Systematic Theology*, vol. I (Chicago: University of Chicago Press, 1951), p. 256, also pp. 235–237.

25. The idealistic distinction between an "empirical" and a "valuating" sense of essence represented an essential element in this definition of creative activity; see Tillich, *Systematic Theology*, vol. I, pp. 202–203. Tillich's statement of the "Protestant principle" and his Christology also served the purpose of assuring continuing new creation by means of the call to abandon outmoded forms of meaning for new possibilities; cf. Tillich, *Protestant Era*, pp. 200–205; *Systematic Theology*, vol. I, p. 134.

26. In 1968 I argued the importance of tracing this shift in Tillich's thought, and I continue to hold this view; see David H. Hopper, *Tillich: A Theological Portrait* (Philadelphia: J. B. Lippincott Co., 1968), pp. 89–100.

27. Tillich, *Courage to Be*, p. 43. Wilhelm Pauck describes the experience in Tillich's life which lies behind this definition of creativity; see Wilhelm and Marion Pauck, *Paul Tillich: His Life and Thought* (New York: Harper & Row, 1976), p. 76.

28. Paul Tillich, *Systematic Theology*, vol. III (Chicago: University of Chicago Press, 1963), p. 68.

29. "Religious-socialism" was the term used by Tillich to describe the program for political and social renewal. Tillich seems to have consistently exaggerated the significance of this small, esoteric movement; see Pauck, *Paul Tillich*, p. 74.

30. Paul Tillich, "Die Theologie des Kairos und die gegenwärtige geistige Lage," *Theologische Blätter*, vol. 23, no. 11 (November 1934), col. 314 (my translation).
31. For an account of this development, see Hopper, *Tillich*, pp. 65–100.
32. In 1934 Tillich identified two types of existentialism: an individualist existentialism deriving from Kierkegaard and a social-historical existentialism deriving from Karl Marx and "Jewish prophecy." Tillich identified with the latter against the former; see Tillich, "Die Theologie des Kairos," col. 309. See also Paul Tillich, "Beyond Religious Socialism," *Christian Century*, vol. 66, no. 24 (June 15, 1944), pp. 732–733.
33. In 1928 Tillich wrote a small piece with the title "Die technische Stadt als Symbol," but this brief article did not break new ground on the subject, generally reflecting his earlier themes.
34. Paul Tillich, "The Person in a Technical Society," in *Christian Faith and Social Action*, ed. John A. Hutchison (New York: Charles Scribner's Sons, 1953), p. 137.
35. It is conceivable that disillusion can also move in the opposite direction, depending upon what may have been the previous focus of hope.
36. Cf. B. F. Skinner, *Beyond Freedom and Dignity* (New York: Alfred A. Knopf, 1971).
37. Tillich, in this context, makes use of insights from Martin Buber, whom he essentially ignored in his earlier thought; see Paul Tillich, *Theology of Culture*, ed. Robert C. Kimball (London: Oxford University Press, 1959), pp. 188–199.
38. Tillich, "The Person in a Technical Society," in Hutchison, *Christian Faith*, pp. 150–151.
39. Ibid., p. 151.
40. Ibid., pp. 151–152.
41. Ibid., p. 137 (emphasis mine).
42. See Pauck, *Paul Tillich*, p. 76. The 1918 date is somewhat uncertain. It occurred during Tillich's "last furlough of the war."
43. The reference is to the use of many of Tillich's ideas in the cause of National Socialism in Germany during the 1930s; see n. 31 above.
44. The paper was to be published in 1964. See Paul Tillich, *The Future of Religions* (New York: Harper & Row, 1966), p. 11.
45. Ibid., pp. 40, 51.
46. Jürgen Moltmann, *The Experiment Hope* (London: SCM Press, 1975), p. 120.
47. Jürgen Moltmann, *The Theology of Hope* (New York: Harper & Row, 1967), p. 33.
48. Ibid., p. 34.
49. Ibid.
50. See Christopher Morse, *The Logic of Promise in Moltmann's Theology* (Philadelphia: Fortress Press, 1979), pp. 3–16.
51. Moltmann, *Experiment Hope*, pp. 33–38.
52. Ibid., p. 33. It should be pointed out that there are important similarities here between the thought of Ernst Bloch and Paul Tillich. Bloch and Tillich knew each other well, though this is only mentioned in passing by Pauck,

Paul Tillich, p. 282. Tillich contributed an essay to a volume in honor of Bloch: *Ernst Bloch zu ehren Beiträge zu seinem Werk,* ed. Siegried Unseld (Frankfurt: Suhrkamp, 1965).

53. Moltmann, *Experiment Hope*, p. 33.

54. Reference is made here to Whitehead's concept of "prehension" which countered the mechanistic positivism of nineteenth-century science. Whitehead argued that what exists at the end of a process, for example, human freedom, must have existed as potentiality at the earliest stages (e.g., the molecular level) of the process; cf. Alfred North Whitehead, *Science and the Modern World* (New York: New American Library of World Literature, Mentor Books, 1948), pp. 73–74, 80–81. Cf. also Alfred North Whitehead, *The Function of Reason* (Boston: Beacon Press, 1958), pp. 20–22.

55. Moltmann, *Experiment Hope*, p. 34.

56. Jürgen Moltmann et al., *The Future of Hope*, ed. Frederick Herzog (New York: Herder & Herder, 1970), p. 11.

57. Ibid., p. 10.

58. Moltmann, *Experiment Hope*, p. 32.

59. Moltmann, *Theology of Hope*, p. 303; see also pp. 334–335.

60. Ibid., p. 338.

61. New York Times, *One Hundred Years of Famous Pages From the New York Times 1851–1951* (New York: Simon & Schuster, 1951), p. xii.

62. Moltmann, *Future of Hope*, p. 10.

63. Here, in the United States, one thinks perhaps of Gordon Kaufman's *Theology for a Nuclear Age* (Philadelphia: Westminster Press, 1985), though this book in no way matches the theological significance of a Tillich or a Moltmann.

64. See above, pp. 73–74, 93–95.

65. Walter M. Abbott, ed., *The Documents of Vatican II* (New York: American Press, 1966), pp. 209, 247. One should not pretend that there is a uniform statement of this view of the church as "the people of God" in the documents of Vatican II. It is rather only suggested at some critical points, especially in the "Pastoral Constitution on the Church in the Modern World," pp. 199–248.

66. In *The Present Age* Kierkegaard speaks paradoxically of two forms of "leveling," one deriving from the pressures of a mass culture involving a loss of individuality and the sense of selfhood, and another initiated by God which "levels" everyone up, as it were, by assuring each person's self-worth in faith; see Søren Kierkegaard, *The Present Age* (New York: Harper Torchbook, 1962) pp. 62, 81–82. Later, Kierkegaard seems to have veered somewhat from this course in stress upon the imitation of Christ.

67. This is especially clear in *The Antichrist* (1888).

68. In speaking of an "aristocratic Christianity" in his *Letters and Papers from Prison* (New York: Macmillan Co., 1971), pp. 318, 345–346, Bonhoeffer gave expression to thoughts which, at the very least, raise cautionary flags; cf. David H. Hopper, *A Dissent on Bonhoeffer* (Philadelphia: Westminster Press, 1975).

69. One can offer the suggestion here that Ernst Troeltsch in his *Social Teachings*

of the Christian Churches may have overstated the significance of natural law in his explanation of the "ecclesiastical civilization" of the Middle Ages, thus failing to appreciate the "sectarian" tendencies in the thought of both Luther and Calvin with their common insistence upon the role of the Holy Spirit in the hearing of the word of God, and in the nurturing of the community of faith.

70. Bonhoeffer, *Letters and Papers from Prison*, p. 336.
71. Walter Kaufmann, ed., *The Portable Nietzsche* (New York: Viking Press, 1954), p. 619.
72. See ch. 3 above.
73. Perhaps the so-called dialogue between the major world religious traditions should always entertain this "third" presence, the secular.
74. H. Richard Niebuhr, in his *Christ and Culture* (New York: Harper & Brothers, Harper Torchbook, 1956), pp. 83–115, discusses this phenomenon under the chapter heading "The Christ of Culture."
75. Lynn White, Jr.'s spiritual odyssey reflects this pattern.
76. Tillich, *Future of Religions*, p. 50.
77. The phrasing comes from the John Allen translation (1813), 7th edition, of John Calvin, *Institutes of the Christian Religion* (Philadelphia: Presbyterian Board of Christian Education), 4.20.3.

Chapter 6: Summation and Theological Postscript

1. Much the same thing can be said of the 1989 turmoil in China.
2. Titoism: the assertion of a national communism in opposition to Soviet control of a world communist movement.
3. This phenomenon is referred to as Eurocommunism, akin to Titoism.
4. Here again, John Diggins' book, *The Lost Soul of American Politics* (Chicago: University of Chicago Press, 1984), proves very instructive.
5. Robert N. Bellah et al., *Habits of the Heart* (Berkeley, Calif.: University of California Press, 1985).
6. *New York Times*, July 27, 1988, p. A25.
7. *Star Tribune* (Minneapolis/St. Paul), Aug. 19, 1988, p. 23A.
8. See Karl Barth's estimate of Calvin in Eberhard Busch, *Karl Barth: His Life from Letters and Autobiographical Texts* (Philadelphia: Fortress Press, 1976), p. 439.
9. Max Weber so argued in *The Protestant Ethic and the Spirit of Capitalism* (1930; reprint, New York: Charles Scribner's Sons, 1958), and more recently, Michael Walzer, in the area of politics, *The Revolution of the Saints* (New York: Atheneum Publishers, 1968).
10. John Calvin and Jacopo Sadoleto, *A Reformation Debate*, ed. John C. Olin (New York: Harper & Row, Harper Torchbook, 1966), p. 58.
11. John Calvin, *Institutes*, trans. Henry Beveridge, vol. II, p. 652 (4.20.2); p. 654 (4.20.4).
12. I have argued this point at greater length in an unpublished paper, "Ecclesiology and Gospel in Calvin: 'process' without 'Process' " (Grand Rapids: H. H. Meeter Center for Calvin Studies, 1986).

13. Martin Bucer, *Instruction in Christian Love* (1523), trans. Paul F. Fuhrmann (Richmond: John Knox Press, 1952), p. 30.
14. This, of course, illumines a dimension of Calvin's teaching on "predestination" different from that which usually comes to mind. It suggests, for example, an alternative to Max Weber's development of that theme in terms of a heightened "anxiety" about God's eternal decree, which then intensified economic activity as search for a sign of God's blessing; see Weber, *Protestant Ethic*.
15. Calvin, *Institutes*, vol. II, p. 282 (4.1.3) (emphasis mine).
16. Ibid., p. 11 (3.7.5). The scripture verse that is key here is 1 Cor. 12:12.
17. Calvin, *Institutes*, vol. I, pp. 471–472 (3.2.4). In the Servetus case, Calvin made the unfortunate decision that a Christian could not learn from one who was himself unteachable.
18. Of note in this connection is the subsequent Calvinist affirmation that, with the ascension of Christ, Christ shares in God's providential governance of history. Of note also is Calvin's interpretation of the "image of God" as it relates to the church and the political order. *Institutes*, vol. II, p. 11 (3.7.6).
19. Calvin, *Institutes*, vol. II, p. 657 (4.20.8).
20. Jane Dempsey Douglass, *Women, Freedom, and Calvin* (Philadelphia: Westminster Press, 1985), p. 22.
21. See Steven Ozment, *The Age of Reform, 1250 to 1550* (New Haven, Conn.: Yale University Press, 1980), p. 271.
22. Calvin, *Institutes*, vol. I, p. 309 (2.7.12); p. 310 (2.7.13).
23. Ibid., vol. II, p. 676 (4.20.32).
24. Darrett B. Rutman, *John Winthrop's Decision for America* (Philadelphia: J. B. Lippincott Co., 1975), p. 100.
25. Ibid., p. 99. Despite his disaffection with Calvinism, Horace Mann, in the nineteenth century, certainly mirrored main features of the Puritan civic ethos; see ch. 1 above.
26. Dietrich Bonhoeffer, *No Rusty Swords* (New York: Harper & Row, 1965), pp. 238–239.
27. Karl Barth, *The German Church Conflict* (Richmond: John Knox Press, 1965), p. 45.
28. Karl Barth, *Community, State, and Church* (Garden City, N.Y.: Doubleday & Co., 1960), pp. 170–171.
29. Ibid., p. 175.
30. The 1960 edition of *Community, State, and Church* has a preface by Will Herberg which fails to discern this source of Barth's thought and the importance of Calvin's "third use of the law"; see pp. 35–37.
31. This point needs to be developed more extensively at another time and place.
32. For the future, an alteration of present patent laws to favor environmental conservation could certainly help to redirect economic effort and inventive purpose.
33. Calvin, *Institutes*, vol. I, p. 676 (4.20.32).

INDEX OF PROPER NAMES

INDEX OF
SUBJECTS